PENNY STOCKS

How to Find Penny Stocks, Day Trading, and Earning Big Money Online

(Top Strategies and Secrets of Penny Stocks Trading)

Thomas Carter

Published by Kevin Dennis

Thomas Carter

All Rights Reserved

Penny Stocks: How to Find Penny Stocks, Day Trading, and Earning Big Money Online (Top Strategies and Secrets of Penny Stocks Trading)

ISBN 978-1-989965-62-7

All rights reserved. No part of this guide may be reproduced in any form without permission in writing from the publisher except in the case of brief quotations embodied in critical articles or reviews.

Legal & Disclaimer

The information contained in this book is not designed to replace or take the place of any form of medicine or professional medical advice. The information in this book has been provided for educational and entertainment purposes only.

The information contained in this book has been compiled from sources deemed reliable, and it is accurate to the best of the Author's knowledge; however, the Author cannot guarantee its accuracy and validity and cannot be held liable for any errors or omissions. Changes are periodically made to this book. You must consult your doctor or get professional medical advice before using any of the suggested remedies, techniques, or information in this book.

Upon using the information contained in this book, you agree to hold harmless the Author from and against any damages, costs, and expenses, including any legal fees potentially resulting from the application of any of the information provided by this guide. This disclaimer applies to any damages or injury caused by the use and application, whether directly or indirectly, of any advice or information presented, whether for breach of contract, tort, negligence, personal injury, criminal intent, or under any other cause of action.

You agree to accept all risks of using the information presented inside this book. You need to consult a professional medical practitioner in order to ensure you are both able and healthy enough to participate in this program.

Table of Contents

INTRODUCTION 1

CHAPTER 1: THE BASICS 4

CHAPTER 2: INVESTING VS. TRADING 18

CHAPTER 3: TRADING PHILOSOPHIES AND APPROACHES 26

CHAPTER 4: TECHNICAL ANALYSIS: THE POSITIVE AND NEGATIVE 40

CHAPTER 5: MYTHS ABOUT PENNY STOCKS 45

CHAPTER 7: LIMITING LOSSES TO INCREASE PROFITABILITY 51

CHAPTER 8: PENNY STOCK BIDDING AND PRICING 56

CHAPTER 9: FUTURE EXPECTATIONS OF TRADING PENNY STOCKS 59

CHAPTER 10: FUNDAMENTAL ANALYSIS 68

CHAPTER 11: TRACKING YOUR PENNY STOCKS 76

CHAPTER 12: ADVANCED STRATEGIES 94

CHAPTER 13: SPOTTING HOT TRENDS IN PENNY STOCKS 103

CHAPTER 14: TECHNIQUES OF TRADING PENNY STOCKS: GETTING SPECIFIC 107

CHAPTER 15: BUYING STOCKS 113

CHAPTER 16: TECHNICAL TRENDS 115

CHAPTER 17: ADVANTAGES AND DISADVANTAGES OF PENNY STOCKS 123

CHAPTER 18: TIPS THAT CAN GET YOU A LONG WAY 134

CHAPTER 19: LEARNING THE BASICS OF DAY TRADING . 140

CHAPTER 20: THE HABIT OF COURAGE 161

CHAPTER 21: PENNY STOCK ANALYSIS TECHNIQUES 165

CHAPTER 22: FINDING YOUR BROKER 179

CONCLUSION 191

Introduction

Penny stocks are stocks, though they differ from the typical stock you'd imagined an investor on Wall Street buying and selling. This is because, like its name suggests, penny stocks are rather small investments. Actually, penny stocks are common stocks that are valued at less than one dollar. Yes, we're talking about stocks with a value of mere cents. This doesn't necessarily mean, though, that penny stocks aren't worth an investor's time, that they aren't worth **your** time. Although their low valuation makes them highly speculative and somewhat volatile, investors such as yourself have the opportunity to make large returns on these small investments. You'll find this type of trading mainly in the US, the UK, and Canada. While these forms of stocks are best known as penny stocks in American and Canada, they are oftentimes referred to as "penny shares" in the UK.

If you are a beginner investor and trader, then penny stocks might be just the right type of trading you need, though trading and investing in penny stocks is not as easy and risk-free as it often seems. Just like other forms of trading, penny stocks can be rather risky but very rewarding. They also become quite exciting when you observe a rise in value, either from a few cents to a few dollars.

In this book, you are going to learn the basics about penny stocks—all the vital and crucial information you need to have a pre-established understanding for **before** you take on the investing process. After introducing the basic outline of penny stocks—what they are, what they do, and how they work—we'll discuss the techniques, strategies, and approaches to technical analysis that will prove useful and beneficial throughout our endeavors with penny stock trading. Having this information readily available will help you develop your trading skills and knowledge, and will increase your investment profitability.

You'll also be introduced to the world of penny stocks, its benefits, its drawbacks, and the analytical approaches you need in order to determine which penny stock investment opportunities are the right ones for **you.** You'll learn where and how to trade penny stocks, the potential risks that come with trading, how you can easily avoid these risks, and, of course, the simple strategies that will help guide you through the process of buying, selling, and managing penny stock investments. Take your time and go through the following chapters of this book to learn everything you need to know about penny stocks and penny stock trading.

Chapter 1: The Basics

Penny stocks are gaining popularity these days, especially among people who are open to investment opportunities. After all, who would not want to make a big profit?

But, what are penny stocks? Are they truly worth investing in?

Penny stocks are also referred to as penny shares or cent stocks. It is worth noting that most penny stocks cost more than a penny or a cent. Years ago, any stock with a price of less than a dollar per share was deemed a penny stock. However, the U.S. SEC revised the definition of a penny stock. Today, any stock that is worth less than $5 per share is a penny stock. Therefore, even if a stock is worth $3, it is still a penny stock. In the U.K., a penny stock is any stock with a price that falls below £1.

Since penny stocks have a relatively low value, they are mostly traded by small companies. But you can still find a few well-established companies that trade penny stocks on major market exchanges.

Is it for you?

Like other investments, trading penny stocks involves risks. There is no guarantee that you will make sums of profit. In fact, there is a probability of losing all your money. And unlike other business ventures, trading penny stocks is a high-risk investment. Now, this cuts both ways: There is a high probability of losing your money, but there is also a chance of making lots of profit. Many successful investors earn more than five times of their initial investment.

If you can invest some money and expect for high returns, if you can take up the challenges of a high-risk investment and spend hours of research and analysis to increase your chances of success, if you can make your own decision and take the opportunity to earn big amounts of money, then investing in penny stocks is for you.

Investing in penny stocks is like playing a game of slots at a casino. You can easily lose everything, but you can also double, triple, and even multiply your money more than 30 times. The glaring difference is that a game of slots is purely speculative. You simply spin the wheel and have no control of anything. The result of the game entirely depends on the machine. When you invest in or trade penny stocks, you will have more control of the "game." You will not be dealing with some random generator. Instead, you will encounter an existing market, businesses, real trends, and real people. There are many factors that you can consider that can help you come up with a wiser investment decision. And, unlike the game of slots which is purely speculative, continuous success in trading penny stocks requires serious efforts, research and analysis, patience, experience and, of course, some good luck.

Investing vs. trading

The terms "investing" and "trading" almost have no difference; but, for the word Nazis out there, "investing" simply means buying penny stocks with a hope that their price will soon increase so you can sell them for a profit, while the term "trading" entails a more active approach. Since the value of penny stocks fluctuates even within a day's time, you can make multiple trades within a short period. In fact, you can make more than 10 trades within a 24-hour timeline.

This book uses both terms synonymously. After all, in making money, how quickly you make a trade or the number of trades that you do in a day does not matter. The only thing that matters is how much profit you have made, if any.

Whether you see yourself as an investor or a trader is up to you. Still, the same principle applies: Buy when the price is low; sell when the price is high.

Penny stocks vs. blue-chip stocks

Penny stocks and blue-chip stocks are both issued by companies. However, there are differences between the two. When you invest in penny stocks, it is important that you understand their differences in terms of:

Volatility

If there is one thing that penny stocks are known for, it is having a high volatility. This means that their prices continuously rise and fall within a short period of time. This is the reason why many investors shy away from penny stocks, but this same reason is also why other investors see penny stocks as a golden opportunity that you can make money from.

Unlike penny stocks, blue-chip stocks have a low volatility. Therefore, if you want to be more secure of your investment and do not want to see drastic changes in the prices of stocks, you would find blue-chip stocks as a better option.

Dividends

Although possible, you should not expect to receive any dividends from penny stocks. If you are a holder of blue-chip stocks, then it is normal to receive dividends from the company.

Sensitivity

Penny stocks are very sensitive. Some minor changes in sector influences can easily affect the prices of penny stocks, causing them to increase or decrease; while blue-chip stocks are not easily affected by external factors and demonstrates more stability.

Speculative

On the one hand, penny stocks have a highly speculative nature. There are many factors that easily affect their prices. On the other hand, blue-chip stocks have more stability and a low speculative value.

Profit potential

Investing in penny stocks has a high-profit potential. It is not uncommon to see experienced traders earning more than five times their initial investment. However, the risk involved is also high. Blue chip stocks are more secure. However, they have a low profit margin. Meaning, you will have to invest a lot of money just to earn a decent amount of profit. And, yes, there is still a risk of losing your investment.

Availability of data

Penny stocks are not as transparent as blue-chips stocks. You will need to do more research to gather information about a particular penny stock. Due to the lack of or poor transparency, you will have less data to analyze and base your decision on. This makes it hard to figure out if you are really making a wise investment decision.

Blue-chip stocks are more open and transparent. Companies usually have an open book of information about their enterprise. This makes it easy for you to find out if the company is doing good or not. Of course, if the business is doing well, the prices of its stocks tend to increase.

High volatility of Penny Stocks

Although it is hard to tell whether the price of a given penny stock will increase or decrease, one thing is sure: All penny stocks have high volatility. Therefore, even if the price of a penny stock decreases today, it can still increase later or tomorrow. However, there is also a chance that it will continuously decrease, which can cause you to lose your investment. When dealing with penny stocks, you should expect to encounter dramatic price swings. This is not completely a bad thing. In fact, this presents an opportunity for you to make money.

First, you should understand what volatility is. Volatility refers to rapid and unpredictable changes in price. Therefore, when we say that penny stocks have high volatility, it means that the prices of penny stocks change quickly and dramatically. A sudden decrease in price today may turn into a huge upswing tomorrow. Such price swings normally happen. So, you should expect for the prices of certain penny stocks to rise and fall almost randomly.

There are many factors that influence the volatility of penny stocks. It is important for you to have an understanding of these factors, so you can come up with a good investment decision.

The Investors

The investors themselves greatly affect the prices of penny stocks. Their activity of buying or selling stocks causes the prices of penny stocks to fluctuate. Unfortunately, this factor is hard to control because investors exercise their own discretion in buying and selling penny stocks.

Reports

Publicly-traded companies submit financial reports regularly. Although these reports are not sufficient to provide you with enough to data in making a good investment strategy, these reports heavily influence the actions and decisions of many investors.

Volatile market

It should not be a surprise that sensitive stocks, such as penny stocks, have a volatile nature considering that the market itself is volatile. The market is not just made of goods or stock certificates; it is composed of and run by real people — people who have their own preferences, interests, and prejudices.

Government laws and policies

To better serve and protect their citizens, as well as for their own benefit, governments take an active interest in businesses. For example, governments usually enact laws and policies to encourage investors to put up a business, so that they can lower their rate of unemployment. Of course, a new business means a new competitor in the market which can affect the performance and market share of other businesses. The taxes imposed by governments upon business enterprises also affect a business. It is worth noting that the prices of penny stocks depend on the performance of the company. If business is good, then the prices of penny stocks of the company tend to increase; however, if the company is experiencing losses, there is a big chance that a drop in the prices of its penny stocks will immediately follow.

Economic problems

Economic problems usually have a strong negative impact on the prices of penny stocks. If left unresolved, these problems can cause a severe drop not only in the prices of stocks but also in the level of quality of life of the people. The economy is a big subject. It affects businesses, investors, the masses, the government, as well as consumer confidence, among other things.

Consumer behavior

How consumers respond to businesses also affects the volatility of stocks. When a business is doing well, the prices of its penny stocks also increase. Unfortunately, consumers usually change their preferences. Although they may be fond of a particular product today does not mean that they will still buy the same product tomorrow. This behavior strongly affects the performance of a business which, in turn, affects the prices of its penny stocks.

Competition

Competition is good, especially for the consumers. It compels businesses to only offer high-quality products and services. However, just as one business dominates the others, the increase in price of its penny stocks is counterbalanced by the decrease in price of other penny stocks belonging to a different company or companies.

These factors, among others, influence the volatility of stocks. With so many factors to consider, including those that are outside your control, it becomes hard to determine whether the price of certain penny stocks will increase or decrease. In fact, even highly experienced traders still commit wrong investment decisions. But do not be discouraged; success is still possible, and there are many traders who are happy with their investments.

Take advantage of price swings

Keep in mind that the key to making profit is by taking advantage of the unavoidable price swings. The key principle remains the same: Buy when the price is low, and sell when the price is high. Although you can make multiple trades in a day, it is not uncommon to wait for the value of your penny stocks to make a substantial increase before selling them.

You can always expect the prices of penny stocks to shoot up; however, if you make a buy order at the wrong time, you may experience a dramatic and continuous decrease in price that even if the price increases in the future, it would not be enough to recoup your initial investment. Therefore, although patience is a virtue, proper timing is also essential.

Chapter 2: Investing Vs. Trading

There is an essential argument when it comes to all stocks; trading versus investing, and what is the better strategy? The answer to this question is not simple, and the truth is that neither method is empirically better than the other. What matters for the individual is that they deal with penny stocks that play to their strengths. For many, this means that they are at their best when they are doing background research into companies. For others, it means that they will do their best when they are following trends and analyzing patterns. For myself, I have made most of my money through trading stock, although I have had several investments pay off in the past. It is more work for me to make a dollar through investing than it is through trading, and that is perhaps the most important aspect to this debate. Both methods produce profit, but the dollar to hour ratio is doing to be far different depending on the individual, not the method. That being said, there is an argument for both main styles of making a profit through penny stocks. Reading the argument for each style, try and figure out what method you would gravitate towards. Your ability to succeed in either method is made from factors of time, resources, investment pool, family commitments, and more. By simply reading how each method works, you should be able to picture what fits more in line with your lifestyle.

An Argument for Investing in Penny Stocks

Investing in a penny stock is the opportunity to get in on the ground floor of a company. You have the ability to buy shares in a company for a very cheap price, and if you just hold onto those shares then you will get paid multiple times your base investment. This idea is at the heart of investing – make a long term bet on a company, and literally help them grow into something successful. This type of transaction makes a lot of sense for those that have a knack for researching a company. It is suited towards people that like to get into the nitty gritty details of a company, like the basic product that they are producing, understanding the market for that product, being realistic about the manufacturing costs, and so on. The more information available to the investor, the more this method makes sense. It is not just important to be informed about the financials of a company, but an investor also needs to be aware of all liabilities that a company holds, and even needs to know a bit about the key people running the company.

This method of making profit from penny stocks should only be practiced on the NYSE. It can also work on the OTCBB, but this is far more risky. For a long term investment, you will want the assurance that comes with trading stock on the NYSE – there is some degree of financial vetting and you can be assured that the documents you are reading about a company are accurate. This method should never be practiced on the pink sheets, as information is too inaccurate to make an accurate predication about the future financial viability of a company.

The methods of investing that I suggest for this method are buy and hold trading, and value trading. I will go into more detail in these more specific methods in the next chapter, but for now know that each will have an investment period of around three months. The total amount that you should be investing in a company using these strategies needs to be fairly large. You want to have investments be around one thousand dollars, which can be fairly steep and limit your ability to invest in other companies. These methods are for those that have faith in a company, and are betting on their ability to predict the future in the market. It almost resembles a science, and this is perhaps the largest argument for this style of investing. You are not so much as making a bet, as much as making an educated guess as to what companies will be successful. The initial cost of investment is very high, for penny stocks, but the potential profits through these methods is many multiples of your base investment. This is particularly true if a company reaches mainstream success, breaking out of a penny stock to become better known on a national level. This is extremely rare, but in these instances an investor can make several hundreds of times their base investment.

An Argument for Trading Penny Stocks

Investing in penny stocks will earn big profit in a matter of months, but penny stock traders can earn profit on a daily basis. Penny stock traders are not quite investors, meaning they do not care about the company whose stock they are buying. They care about the volatility of the stock, or the amount of change that stock undergoes in some interval of time. For example, I might trade company ABC because their stock has seen a volatility of thirty percent for the last five days. This means that the company's stock has seen fluctuations of thirty percent each day for five days — these movements are not always in one direction, but there is a trend of rapid shifts with company ABC. In this example, I don't care about what ABC produces, as I will never be involved in company ABC for long enough that they ever make a product that I see.

The type of research that a penny stock trader conducts is entirely around the volatility and trends of a stock. It requires far less research because the type of information that investors buy stock on is not meant to affect the stock price in matter of weeks or months, but in a matter of hours. Traders invest in a company and will typically cash out the very same day. They are only getting involved in a company so they can reap the benefits of changes in the stock price as they take place over the course of one trading day.

There are many arguments for penny stock trading over investing, but the strongest ones are that this method does not require market specific knowledge, penny stocks are inherently unreliable for investing, and trading penny stocks opens the effective number of exchanges you can be involved with. The first of these arguments is strong; you don't need to know anything about the market that a company is producing a product in, nor do you even need to know what the company is producing. Essentially, no knowledge is needed about any sector of the economy, as this will have a negligible impact on trading. The second argument is certainly true as well; penny stocks are risky investments. Even on the OTCBB, you never know what financial documents you are looking at have been embellished, are completely truthful, or are flagrantly false. It makes planning a long term investment very tricky because you can never trust the company line. The third argument is perhaps the most important; it is true that trading opens up the exchange that you can invest in. While I would never suggest that you trade on the pink sheets, you should have little to no problem trading on the OTCBB. This offers the perfect amount of real time information and has enough market volatility for a trader. An investor would want to be highly selective and instead trade on the NYSE, requiring larger capital investment and limiting the stocks that they can invest in to the small pool located on the NYSE. These arguments combined paint a picture of trading being a great avenue to get into the stock market for those with small pools of capital, and those with little market knowledge.

Chapter 3: Trading Philosophies And Approaches

There are several different approaches that you can take to trading. None of these philosophies are necessarily more profitable than any other one, but you will likely want to find one or two approaches that work for you and stick to those. Trading is done on a learning curve, and the more you experiment and take notes on your trades, the better you will do in the long run. I have organized the following methods of trading by effectiveness in penny stock trading. As you begin to practice, start with the first method and move down form there. Take a good look at any situation and you will be able to use one of these four methods to make a profit.

Swing Traders

Swing traders make their money by identifying trends, and purchasing a stock when the market overreacts to a trend and course corrects, but the tend is in fact still going. A typical stock that follows this pattern will see low prices every three to four trading days. It is at this time when traders believe a stock is being overvalued. The stock sells off for a low price, and then the stock price increases because other traders believe the trend is still continuing. These trends have nothing to do with the actual product that any of these companies produce, but are rather an indication of how other traders feel about a particular company.

This is the type of trading that I do, and I believe this is my preferred method of trading because it keeps money coming in very regularly and yet I have a few days, or even weeks, to analyze a trend before I decide whether or not I am going to buy a stock. You do not need to purchase a stock the first time the price falls because stocks that fall under this category will have five, six, maybe even seven swings in high volatility. This gives you time to look at a stock and notice if a pattern is forming.

The gamble that you take on swing trades is whether or not a cycle will continue. You will always be purchasing when the stock is at a low price, but your investment is a statement saying you are confident that the trend is still continuing and that the price will go up again. These cycles do stop, and while it's possible for them to persist for a month or two, false cycles are identified all the time. Diversification will be discussed later in this book, but as a general rule you can never be too sure if you are buying in the middle of a cycle, or if the cycle has ended, so you will need to purchase multiple stocks that you think are cycling to ensure that at least some of these bets pay off.

The real downside to swing trading is in the research it requires and the time investment in this research. The trends that you are analyzing all come from stock prices and no underlying information about the value of a company so all of the research is incredibly dry, full of stock prices and virtually no other information about products, people, or even objectives of the company. You are also unsure of how often a cycle repeats – although a cycle is typically three or four days, it can be much longer or shorter. For research purposes, this means not just looking at many stocks, but also viewing this data in a variety of ways to create a picture that identifies a cycle. If you are dealing in time frames that are either too long or too short then you will not be identifying the cycles as they happen. You will need a decent amount of time to dedicate to research for swing trading, but you will never be rushed to buy as these trends take course over a long enough period of time that you have the option to thoroughly weigh your choices and make a well informed decision.

Day Traders

Day traders make their money on short held trades. This means that they are buying and selling stock numerous times throughout the day. There are a couple barriers to entry for day traders that might make this approach unappealing or infeasible. For one, day trading is a full time job. It requires six to eight hours in a given day, and for each moment you will need to be paying attention to market trends. Two, day traders require either a broker that has a very low price per trade, or are making trades large enough that they can overcome the money lost by simply conducting the trade. Each trade will cost you some amount of money, and even with the cheapest brokers this amount is typically five dollars or more. This might seem like a small amount, but on each and every trade you need to clear ten dollars before you are starting to see a profit. When you are making thirty cents per share on a trade, you might end up having to buy many more shares than you would like just to cover the cost of your broker.

If you have the time to work on day trading, then there are a few core tenants to follow to ensure that you stay ahead of your competition. You will be making money on the quick rise and fall of a stock. You will want to keep an eye on a stock and look for the intervals in which it is falling and rising. You know that you want to buy low an sell high, but your strategy to should be to pick up on these patterns before your competitors do – this means taking a risk that you believe you saw a pattern before a majority of other traders.

Another tenant to day trading is that you must never concern yourself about what an actual company produces, or to a lesser extent, if they are even legitimate. You are earning money by the minute, and the numbers and metrics for each company will be far more important to you. The only time you should concern yourself about a company outside of its bars and graphs is if a sudden major news story appears and it will affect the price right away. For penny stocks however, this is extremely uncommon. Most of these companies will not be recognized in the news and the central pieces of data that you will be dealing with are the minute-to-minute index prices. Aspects of a company like portfolios, financial investments – you will not have time to look at these, nor should you care about what the documents say.

Some advantages of day trading are that you have an up to date record how much money you are making. At the end of every week you can go over your financials on a day-to-day basis to see how well you are doing. You can even calculate how much money you are making per hour, a feature that cannot be calculated as easily in any other approach to trading. Having this sort of instant feedback is great, but it also comes with the downside of added stress. Day trading is an exhausting job – you must constantly be paying attention to intangible data like index prices, far removed what any company is producing. This can gnaw at the brain over a period of time and can cause added stress and worry about trades. Dealing in cycles, even if they are minute to minute, is a stressful way of earning profit and you will know within a week of trying day trading whether or not you are up for the mental exhaustion that accompanies fast paced trading.

Value Traders

Value trading is somewhat similar philosophically to buy and hold trading, which will be discussed further into the chapter, but the profit can be seen much more quickly and I find the inherit risk for low capitalized investors to be much more acceptable. The strategy that value traders follow is they invest in stocks that are absolutely worth more than they are trading for. This sounds like a trick, like it is the goal of every investor to be doing exactly this, however the difference is the value of the company is calculated based on its underlying assets. Think about it like this, if Apple was trading at $4 a share, and had a total of 1,000 shares available on the exchange, that would mean it has a market capitalization of $4,000. Now this is an extreme example, but anyone can look at this and see that overall Apple is worth more than $4,000. This has nothing to do with it having good employees or strong brand recognition, but rather that it owns physical property that is simply worth more than $4,000. The value of the stock will have to go up because it is a remarkable error that Apple would be priced so low. If we take this concept and apply it to penny stocks, we form the basis for the strategy that you will be using.

You will want to only be looking at stocks listed on the NASDAQ and OTCBB exchanges, since the financial reporting for each company listed is the determinate for whether or not you buy a company. Compare the on paper value to the market capitalization and buy based on undervalued companies. You do not have a guarantee that a stock will go up, but chances are that it will have to, especially if the discrepancy is large enough, typically defined as larger than 5%.

When dealing with penny stock companies you will need to pay extra attention to their financial reporting. Instances of fraud are greatly exaggerated, but they do happen at a greater rate than with companies listed on traditional exchanges. The key to sifting through these financial documents is to look for provable assets, like property. Companies may list assets like patents, but their evaluation was likely done in house and likely is exaggerated, meaning the stock price is not undervalued but trading at the correct price. You will also want to be on the lookout for specific names. Keep track of the CEO, CFO, and names of others in high-ranking positions. You will want to do a little bit of research into these people and see if they come from a strong entrepreneurial background. Entrepreneurs are the determining factor in whether or not a company will be successful – they will ultimately drive the stock price up, not the underlying idea for a product. Ideas are a dime a dozen, but it is the execution that you care about. Look for the assets and pay attention to the management — use this information to determine if a company is truly undervalued.

Buy And Hold Traders

The philosophy of buy and hold trading works far better for traditional exchanges than it does for penny stocks, but on occasion some of the largest profits can be gained from buy and hold trades. These trades rely on buying a stock and holding onto it until it jumps in value. Your picks are decided by doing research into a company's product and financials. You are vetting a company to decide if it has a chance to succeed, and then investing based on your conclusions.

I would be extremely careful using a buy and hold method for penny stocks. Most of these companies will go bust before they ever make one hundred dollars of income. If you go this route you will also be doing an incredible amount of research into each and every company that you look into. You will not be able to filter out companies based on data from the exchanges, and will instead be forced to act on the independent financials and underlying product. Finding this information is usually pretty easy, but depending on the exchange the financial information could be entirely faked. Trading on the NASDAQ and OTCBB, these stocks will have financial documents that are true, unless major fraud is being committed, but the point is that the companies at least met some minimum standards to be listed on these exchanges. If you are trading on Pink Sheets, then there is absolutely no guarantee about any piece of financial information you find on a company. You might think this is absurd — how can a company in America lie so easily — the answer is that they are so small that no one ever notices. If you use a buy and hold strategy you will want to always trade on the NASDAQ and OTCBB. Avoid the Pink Sheets at all costs and never trust any information provided by a company listed on this unregulated exchange. An additional disadvantage is that to earn a good profit on one of these trades you'll need to invest quite a bit of money. A large bet like this is never recommended with penny stocks, and unfortunately diversification is not as easy when using a buy and hold strategy. Since you are betting on a single company, and even if you spread that out across ten companies, you will need a large enough investment in each stock to cover your loses from the stocks that will likely fail. This requires a large amount of capital and just adds to the risk and complications of buy and hold trading around penny stocks.

I might sound bleak about the buy and hold strategy, but when it pays off, it really pays off. It is possible that you get in on the ground floor of a company that will one day be very successful. You could earn thousands, hundreds of thousands, or even millions of dollars this way. It will take a lot of research, a fine assessment of some small companies, and a little bit of luck, but I've had acquaintances that used this method and have made a small fortune. Paydays for buy and hold trades can be many moths off, so even if you do decide to try this strategy, you will still want to try others so you can make some more immediate income.

Chapter 4: Technical Analysis: The Positive And Negative

Technical Analysis is concerned with the method of evaluating securities. This is done by analyzing statistics produced by market activity like past volume and prices. In order to identify patterns that can propose future activity, technical analysts often employ the use of charts and tools but they do not attempt to measure the intrinsic value of a security.

Technical Analysis and Penny Stocks

After all studies have been completed, technical Analysis is often used in penny stocks to determine the right price to sell or buy. So in a nutshell, Technical Analysis is all about predicting price movement. The volume of trade activity, price, trading, and history of such financial vehicles is revealed by the charts of your target stock, the sector of stock you are interested in and the stock market itself.

In successful penny stock investing, the investor must try as much as possible to understand complete fundamental data, technical charts, basic solid chart patterns, experience and basic technical indicators which can be incorporated to determine the real, perceived current value and potential of a penny stock that will make it a future rocket stock.

THE POSITIVE SIDES OF TECHNICAL ANALYSIS

Ease of Observing Buy/Sell Activity

Patterns of buy/sell activity and share values can be easily observed with time especially when technical charts are viewed in concert with other technical indicators.

Provides the Investor with an Insight of Past History

Through technical analysis, the investor gets to know more about the share value trends i.e. how the shares of a stock have been trading in the past. This presents a very important means of understanding and evaluating the current value shares of the stocks.

No Need for Research after All

Supposedly, all fundamental factors affecting the value of a penny stock are already figured into the charts thereby making it very easy for an investor to quickly discern the trends of the value of a stock value without having to do any research whatsoever on the various types of fundamental data that affect the stock.

Gives an Investor a Genuine Understanding of the Stock's Value

Technical Analysis is crucial in helping penny stock traders to understand the value of their stock. In comparison to what they were and what they could be in future. It also helps him to know if the value of the stock genuinely appears to be a solid bargain at the present trading price.

Helps the Trader Predict a New Trend

The buy vs. sell trader activity and trading volume are all included on the charts. All these allow the trader to easily predict a trend reversal, a new trend and the strength of such trends. So, to achieve the greatest potential profit, timely entry and exit points can be potentially predicted.

Creates a Significant Double Confirmation of a Future Trend

It often helps to establish trend reversal for buying or selling especially when potential trends that correspond with fundamentals are revealed by basic technical data as well as presents a significant double confirmation of a future trend. Extraordinary investors greatly value such technical confirmations of fundamental data which are aimed at achieving explosive profits when trading penny stocks.

Useful In Tracking and Figuring Buy and Sell Movement of a Stock

Through Technical Analysis, the history price and volume of a stock can be easily identified. In fact, it helps to reveal the patterns of trading thresholds for a particular period of time so as to be able to obtain the average price movement of a stock. Technical indicators and triggers can also be used to determine the buy and sell movement of a stock and to determine the actual and potential price movement for the future.

Chapter 5: Myths About Penny Stocks

It is obvious that there will be many myths surrounding a topic. It is the same case with penny stocks. There are many myths that surround it and it is important for you to understand them and separate the facts in order to invest in them. We will look at the different myths in this chapter and help you understand the topic better.

It is not easy to buy and sell these stocks

There is widespread misconception that it is difficult to buy and sell these penny stocks. It is believed that you need to be an avid investor or quite well established in order to trade in these stocks. But this is only a misconception. It is known that penny stocks are a bit elusive but that does not make them a hard sell. If you know how to trade in them and are well versed with the concept of paper trading then it will be a cakewalk for you. You will only be required to understand the functioning of these penny stocks and will be good to go.

Big companies were once penny

There is a general belief that big companies like Microsoft were once penny stocks are now billion dollar companies. That is not true. Not every company goes from being a penny stock to a regular stock. If the company is big then they will be listed with a big per share value. Penny stocks are generally for small companies that don't have a big market cap. But that does not mean they cannot be traded in large volumes. There is no such limit of the number of buyers and sellers that can trade with it in a single day. If the stock has gained popularity then many investors will be willing to invest in it regardless of whether it is a small or a micro company.

Penny stocks are frauds

Many new investors will think that these stocks are only fraudulent. They will think so based on the low price of these stocks and how slow some of them move. In fact, many times, the volumes of these stocks will be so low that suspicion will be bound to arise. But, it is baseless to think that way. The stock market encourages all types of stocks. Right from those that are listed at $100 a piece to those that are listed below $5. It does not really matter how small or big the company is. Not saying there might not be any frauds but their presence will be very small in the market.

Prices won't dip further

Don't make the mistake of thinking that prices of these stocks will not dip in the future. There is no lower limit on some stocks. It might keep dipping and then get delisted. So don't think that the price of a stock will not fall any further. If you are confident that despite a dip it is still a good company to invest in then you should go ahead with it. But if you are not confident in the stock then it is best to steer clear off of it.

Prices surely rise up

No. There is no guarantee that the prices that have dipped will surely rise up. It depends on the demand and supply of the stocks and how many are traded in the market. There is no point in waiting on a stock for too long. If the price has not risen then you must dispose it off at the earliest.

Penny stocks are safe bets

Many people believe that it is a safe option to invest in penny stocks. However, there are certain risks involved with penny stocks. You have to understand these risks and only then invest in these stocks. To be honest, there is no investment option in this world that is free of risk. So it is a little unfair to assume that penny stocks will be safe bets. You have to identify the stocks that are good investments and stick with them. This will be possible after a while and once you have studied the market for a few months/ years.

You need to be an insider

There is misconception that you have to be an insider of the company to buy or know about the stocks. But that is not true. You can be an outsider and still know about the best stocks to invest in. If it is a little tough to buy the stocks owing to higher buyer and lower seller volumes then you have to look for the best opportunity when you can enter with the stock. Again, experience will help you out and let you know when the best time to invest in the market is.

It is best to invest in unknowns

Do not make the mistake of investing in unknown companies thinking that it will be a good bet. Nothing is guaranteed in the stock market and it will not be a good idea to invest in a company that is up and coming. What if it turns out to be a bad company or one that is a slow mover? You don't want to remain invested with such a company. So, the best thing is to invest in something that is doing well or has a good track record.

I'm better off without them

No. This is a myth that you should fight away. If you think it is not a good idea to include penny stocks in your portfolio then you are wrong. Penny stocks might be low priced stocks but they will help in diversifying your portfolio. In fact, they are capable of giving you bigger and better profits as compared to your regular stocks. So don't make the mistake of thinking of them as being any less worthy. They are quite worthy and will help you expand your profit margins.

These are the different myths on the topic and it is important for you to understand these thoroughly if you wish to make it big in the world of penny stocks. You can go through these again if you think you need to understand the topic a little better.

Chapter 7: Limiting Losses To Increase Profitability

As an investor, it is pretty much inevitable to come across losing stocks. But the level at which these will damage your portfolio depends on how you will handle them. Basically, there are 3 ways to do this:

Price Barriers

A price barrier is a level at which a share price has a hard time falling through e.g. a lower trend line or a support level. Identifying a barrier price can be done through personal research or professional investment research.

For instance, the shares of XYZ can sink up to 1 dollar level a couple of times but can always bounce back and never go below a dollar. This basically means that they may have a support level at a dollar.

Support levels exist due to the stronger buying pressures at the prices compared to the selling prices which ensures that the share price remains at or above the support. Once you identify the support level, go ahead and place your order to buy shares close to the support level but a bit above.

Assuming that you want to buy 2000 penny stocks of a company XYZ at $1.03- the most effective way to go about it would be to closely monitor the penny stock until it hit a dollar and then begin moving higher to confirm that the support level has been held. After you've confirmed this, put an order to buy shares when they rise away from the dollar.

Stop Loss Orders

A stop loss order is an order to a broker to buy or sell a stock once it reaches a specific price. It is specially designed to limit your loss on a security position.

Just after you get your hands on your shares, put a stop loss order right away below the support level. If the shares rise in value, you continue holding them but when they move to or below the level of your stop loss order then the sell order is activated and your shares are sold at the price therein.

For instance, for our XYZ shares, you would place a stop loss for the 2000 shares at $0.98. If the share price falls below or to $0.98 then this is where your stop loss order kicks in and you end up selling the shares at a loss of approximately 4% plus commissions.

When the support level stays intact and the price of the penny stock maintains above a dollar, then you will have profitably purchased in very near the short term bottom in terms of price. Basically, you will be in a profit's position when the share price travels higher together with the extra insurance of the support level which is just under your position.

You should therefore, adjust your stop loss order upwards if the price of the penny stock happens to rise. For instance, if the price goes past $1.20, you should move your stop order loss to around $1.09 and when they rise past $1.4 then you should increase your stop order loss to $1.29. This strategy will help keep your profits assured. You will be taking advantage of the price rise and your penny stocks will get sold the first time only that the company XYZ's stock price drops.

Making good use of stop loss orders has guaranteed the trading profit of quite a number of penny stock portfolios despite simply winning about only 30% of trades. The reason behind this is that the 70% losing trades were really limited and the gains were allowed to ride hence they exceeded the minimal losses.

Setting up a stop loss price:

When setting up a stop loss price, volatility is something you should highly consider. You really don't want to 'stopped out'. This just means that when the price sinks to the level of your stop order and your shares are sold and then the prices rise right away after the sale into a much more profitable zone.

When you place the opening stop loss order below the support level, it means that you have lessened the possibility of being stopped out in the beginning. Nevertheless, placing your stops correctly gets really complicated when you follow a price that is rising. You will need to decide on your own stop levels based on the penny stocks volatility, your personal investment style and the momentum of the share price trend.

The methodologies here will be best applicable if you have invested about $1,500 or more for each penny stock to minimize the commission cost as a percentage of the total investment value.

If you apply all strategies mentioned in this book, investing in penny stocks will be a bliss for you.

Chapter 8: Penny Stock Bidding And Pricing

Penny Stock Bidding can be a risky investment but having sound knowledge will help you through the entire investment journey. Understanding penny stock bidding and pricing is thus very vital. Since penny stocks have various prices that they can be sold or bought with, it is imperative to understand the following;

1. Bid versus Asking

The price a person is willing to pay for the stock or security is the bid. It is also the number at which you sell your stock if you decide to. The asking price, on the other hand, is the amount of money one is willing to sell your stock/ security at. If you want to purchase stock, it is important to provide accurate bid price whereas if you want to sell stock, you need to know the right asking price.

2. The Spread

The spread is referred to as the difference between the bid and the asking price in a stock sale. This number is a 'build in loss' and it is a fact that one needs to take into considerations the cost of his stock together with many other factors such as transactional fees and the broker's commission. You need to know the right amount of money to ask so as to break even.

3. Two Prices?

Penny stocks are listed with two bid and two ask prices often known as inside and outside ask and bid prices. It is the range at which the stock can be sold and bought

4. Mark Up Pricing

Some dealers or brokers will mark up the price of stock/security to some degree, analyze and maintain an inventory of the product. This is done to keep stock sufficient to both the supply and demand that is out for liquid and orderly markets. This is more likely to be an additional cost and should be taken care of in the build in the cost factor.

Chapter 9: Future Expectations Of Trading Penny Stocks

There will absolutely be some pretty noticeable expected differences when it comes to trading penny stocks in the years and decades to come. Unfortunately, it is also expected that one thing will never change, no matter how much trading practices change, and that this fact will continue to burn investors more than all of the other factors – the human proclivity toward greed. Some things may never change, but the expected positive differences to come in penny stock trading include:

These differences will not necessarily mimic the past as they have done, which in and of itself is a fairly big difference.

It is expected that penny stock investments will become much more mainstream.

Penny stock investments are expected to start to slough off a lot of the negative overtones that currently surround them.

It is expected that penny stocks will provide higher quality methods of investor protection.

Penny stocks are expected to provide more and easier access to the information concerning their underlying companies.

SEEING INTO THE 7 FUTURES OF PENNY STOCKS

Penny stocks are already being noticed more and more as legitimate investments, and they will only gain in popularity - especially with the newer traders who are less experienced. The negative overtones that surround penny stocks will still remain with the big-wigs on Wall Street and the institutional investors, but there will be a quiet group of people who will consistently make their smaller profits by investing in penny stocks.

Tools such as literature and guides on penny stock trading will enable regular investors to learn about and to start investing in penny stocks, and then profit from trading in penny stocks.

Investors of penny stocks will be able to protect themselves better from the now common pitfalls associated with penny stocks. This will largely be due to an influx in the availability of educational materials on the subject. This information will also allow investors to better avoid scams, bad stock picks, and dangerous investments with more ease.

This one is a no-brainer, but a large number of penny stock investors will actually fail to educate themselves or take the time to research the necessary information. Instead, these investors will haphazardly dump money into the penny stocks they get wind of from a friend, at work, or read about in chat rooms. These investors will only lose money.

While reporting requirements and the information available on penny stocks becomes more readily available, the amount of information won't be able to compete with the amount of information that is available for more common and conventionally held stocks.

Investors are just about to enter into a possible lost decade in which the stock market will trade sideways for years to come. Profits will not come from the majority of companies, but only from very specific companies.

The majority of traders will inevitably get burned when another Enron surfaces, or a 'dot-com' bubble, or a Bre-X, or a mortgage meltdown, et cetera. This will happen. In the meantime, a small number of penny stock investors will make a small killing on underlying stocks, and the public will not ever hear about this or hear from those investors directly.

5 PENNY STOCKS TO WATCH AS 2017 APPROACHES

Trading in the penny stock market definitely requires a specific trading skill set to offset the laundry list of inherent risk involved. The following is a composite list of some of the penny stocks you may want to keep your eye on. For the sake of clarity, this book is by no means endorsing, promoting, or otherwise trying to sell you on any one of these penny stocks, but is instead offering them as an example of stocks that you may be interested in looking into. In alphabetical order they are:

Cemtrex Inc. (CETX) – This company makes electronic and industrial and equipment for a wide variety of uses. Cemtrex is currently showing healthy growth in both its monitoring devices and its greenhouse gas devices. This company's stock went public in the year 1990 in the mid-60s range and then fell dropped off of a cliff down to 12 cents in 2004. The next decade brought with it a series of bounces. Cemtrex then rallied in August of 2016 and pulled all the way back to $3.70. The stock paused there for about 6 weeks, just ahead of a bounce which may end up testing, for the 7th time, the big barrier.

This stock has just reported a really strong quarter and has raised forward guidance, which means that sales are expected to rise to around 10% above consensus. This stock could absolutely be in the running for a breakout which may reach double digits eventually.

Cogentix Medical Inc. (CGNT) — This Company sells as well as manufactures and designs such medical devices as urology and endoscopic devices. This company has, since 1993, traded on the public exchanges, and became public at $85; then hit a horrible downtrend that was definitely not pretty which finally ended in 2001. Cogentix rallied its way hard throughout the next 10 years and was sold in the mid-20s. A secondary decline then started in 2008 which dropped this stock to lowest lows it had ever seen. However, Cogentix rallied back again — this time at 50% and peaked at $1.99 per share - when the company signed a purchase agreement in 2016 with a hedge fund in September 2016. All of this was followed up by sideways price action for 7 weeks. Cogentix is now holding brand new 50 and 200 day EMA support and trading at within $0.25 of its rally high.

Origin Agritech Ltd. (SEED) – In 2006, this company actually enjoyed an all-time high of $18.35 and then in it, unfortunately, went into a steep spiral which finally settled in March of 2009 at $1.94. Origin Agritech's ensuing wave of recovery posted a bit of a lower high in 2010 at $15.02, right before it hit an even bigger downward spiral (than in 2009) in 2012. Origin Agritech's stock has since been building a support pattern of resistance above $3.25 and around $1.10. This stock rallied against resistance yet again in September of this year (2016) and then managed to pull back with its price action in the most recent four weeks or so staying just under 50 cents below its breakout level. The upside for this stock after a breakout really has the potential to be significant, effectively lifting the stock to a much stronger resistance at an even $7.00.

PetroQuest Energy Inc. (PQ) – At the turn of the millennium, PetroQuest started trading in single digits on the public exchanges in single digits and then managed to hold support at $5.00, which gained momentum and became a strong uptrend which reached its record high in July 2008 at $116.72. During the economic collapse, this stock really broke down to $2.44 per share, but very quickly bounced up into double digits. This rally faded in 2011 before a soft downtrend that ended up sinking even lower in 2015. This decline in 2015 actually broke the record low of 2009. In March, however, the stock did jump back up above that level, which signaled a possible bottom. This stock's first recovery wave had stalled at $3.60 in May, before an October breakout that will be testing its brand new support at 200-day EMA. When that has been accomplished, PetroQuest's rally is in perfect position in order to tackle the resistance at $4.35 which was created by the breakdown in November 2015.

Xenith Bankshares Inc. (XBKS) – A Virginia-based company, Xenith Bankshares Inc. became public in 2002 at close to $280 and then really rallied to its record high in May of 2006 at just above $360 in May 2006. After all of that, though it went into a horrifying downward spiral and dropped to its record low in March of 2009 at just $0.36 per share. The company's ensuing recovery wave lost steam at the beginning of 2010 at just above $2.00 which gave way to another downward trend in October of 2012 that set a new low for the company. Xenith Bankshares' stock returned to its glory of the 2015 high in August 2016 and then pulled back. This stock, with high odds, will base somewhere above the 50-day EMA and then rally to the resistance, completing its breakout with a moving target nearing $4.00.

Chapter 10: Fundamental Analysis

Once you have created a trading plan and chosen a complimentary trading style, the next thing that you are going to want to consider when it comes to choosing penny stock investments successfully is how you are going to gather data to determine which penny stocks you are going to want to go pursue closely and which you are going to want to give a wide berth. While there are plenty of so-called experts hawking surefire ways to tell good penny stocks from bad, the truth of the matter is that there are only two main ways to go about doing so, fundamental analysis and technical analysis and the details for each will take up the next two chapters. Technical analysis focuses almost exclusively on the current price of the stock in question because it assumes that the current price factors in everything else that is relevant to the penny stock while fundamental analysis delves into the details of the underlying company.

The primary tenants of fundamental analysis state that the whole story of a particular stock can be found if you dig deep enough while technical analysis believes that market movement provides you with all of the details that you need to know. Of the two, it is recommended that new traders start with fundamental analysis before moving on to technical analysis as, while it requires plenty of research, all of the underlying concepts at play are going to be straightforward and easy for almost anyone to understand. The biggest downside of fundamental analysis is that it can often be quite time intensive and once you have looked into the historical precedent you are often stymied by the fact that new relevant information is frequently only released a few times per year. On the other hand, technical analysis can often be completed quite quickly, especially by those who have experience in the field, though it can take a significant amount of study before the concepts at play in this type of analysis become readily apparent.

Performing fundamental analysis

When using fundamental analysis, you are looking to the past to determine the most likely future with the end result of determining the best point to jump onto a new penny stock. When getting started, you are going to want to find all of the information on the penny stock company you are interested in investing in. Once you have everything you need you will want to consider the following:

Establish a baseline: In order to begin analyzing the fundamentals, the first thing that you will need to do is to create a baseline regarding the company's overall performance. In order to generate the most useful results possible, the first thing that you are going to need to do is gather data both regarding the company in question as well as the related industry as a whole. When gathering macro data, it is important to keep in mind that no market is going to operate in a vacuum which means the reasons behind specific market movement can be much more far reaching than they first appear. Fundamental analysis works because of the stock market's propensity for patterns which means if you trace a specific market movement back to the source you will have a better idea of what to keep an eye on in the future.

Furthermore, all industries go through several different phases where their penny stocks are going to be worth more or less overall based on general popularity. If the industry is producing many popular penny stocks, then overall volatility will be down while at the same time liquidity will be at an overall high. As this level of popularity cannot be sustained indefinitely, things will eventually move into a bust period where volatility increases as liquidity decreases.

Consider worldwide issues: Once you have a general grasp on the current phase you are dealing with, the next thing you will want to consider is anything that is going on in the wider world that will after the type of businesses you tend to favor in your penny stocks. Not being prepared for major paradigm shifts, especially in penny stocks where new companies come and go so quickly, means that you can easily miss out on massive profits and should be avoided at all costs.

To ensure you are not blindsided by news you could have seen coming, it is important to look beyond the obvious issues that are consuming the 24-hour news cycle and dig deeper into the comings and goings of the nations that are going to most directly affect your particular subsection of penny stocks. One important worldwide phenomenon that you will want to pay specific attention to is anything in the realm of technology as major paradigm shifts like the adoption of the smartphone, or the current move towards electric cars, can create serious paradigm shifts that can last for multiple years until the technology is completely assimilated.

Look for historical precedents: Once you have a firm grasp on the present and a hypothetical grasp on the future you are going to need to look to the past to see how it measures up. Looking back to how the industry you are considering has done historically will give you a better idea of the true strength of the current phase. When things are starting to look up you can expect that credit will become easier to come by and erratic market movement is at a relative low which means it should be quite easy to turn a profit in nearly all sectors. This will only continue for so long, however, and the longer it does so the more likely it will be to teeter towards a bust at any moment. Remember, this is not a question of if things will turn around once more, but when they will do so.

Look into volatility: When it comes to determining the likely level of volatility that a new company is going to exhibit, the best place to look is to related penny stocks in the same general category. The lower the risk that ancillary stocks exhibit, the lower the chance that the new stock will exhibit aberrant behavior. A lower chance doesn't mean no chance, however, and as a rule of thumb it is important to always assume that volatility could spike, just to be safe. When it comes to penny stocks, planning for the worst and hoping for the best is often the most reliable way to turn a profit. A good barometer for such is the current price when compared to the phase and the current state as compared to the historical point when a bust phase is the most likely to occur.

Trade at the right times: When the time comes to experience a growth phase from the start, the best way to take advantage of it to the fullest is to start with penny stock companies that have the most reliable fundamentals possible. Penny stocks that are already more likely to be viable are going to naturally be a good choice during boom phases as they are statistically more likely to yield positive returns. They also remain a good choice if you are in a bust phase as they are likely going to still be sold for higher rates when compared with assets that are weaker overall.

Chapter 11: Tracking Your Penny Stocks

Even if you don't decide to trade and play the exchange every day, you should at least take the time to track your stocks to prevent surprise drops in the market. You can set many different alerts on your online profiles, but it is still important to see what your stocks are doing and whether you need to make different choices than the alarms you have set for yourself. Sometimes stocks will go stagnant, and that may be a good time to go ahead and sell even if you haven't yet reached your twenty or thirty percent return because often that stagnant information precedes a drop in value for a stock. You also want to see how the stocks that you are tracking are performing to know whether they may be contenders once they reach their fifty-second week. Once you have down the research and purchase part of penny stocks, tracking truly becomes the most important aspect of playing the market.

Tracking stocks is a highly vital skill that will help increase your chances of profiting and maximizing your return on investment. The stock market fluctuates on an hourly basis, and because of that, you can turn profits into losses in the blink of an eye. Therefore it is pertinent to correctly track stocks with the knowledge of what each column represents and how it relates to your specific stock. If for some reason you are found without the use of the internet you can grab the newspaper and track assets from the previous day in the finance section. You also should be able to review most of the information we are providing in your online profile on your brokerage website. We will take the time in this chapter to discuss how to find the stock information, how to understand the information you are viewing, and how to look for patterns when you are tracking your investments.

Finding Your Stock Information

Before you can begin to track the stocks you have purchased and the ones you are considering for investment, you have to be able to find your stock information. The process, online, is relatively straightforward but without the knowledge of where and what to look for, you may find yourself searching through mounds of data. You want first to go into your personalized section of your firm's website where you do all of your purchasing and look for the tracking section of the site, or you can go online to the major news sites and track your stocks through there. You may end up doing a mixture of both depending on where you are and how much time you have to track. They also have started to make apps for your phone that will give you real-time data on the stock market, though some of them do not include penny stocks yet.

Symbols

The next thing you need to do in order to track your stocks is to figure out what the ticker symbol for your particular stocks are. The ticker symbol is a mixture of up to five letters that usually resembles the name of the company or its major product line. These abbreviations are how the stock market tracks each and every business in their system. An example of one of these symbols is Apple which has a ticker symbol of APPL. These symbols should be tracked at the time you choose to purchase them so writing them down will help eliminate this part. However, if you didn't write them down, you can quickly search for the name either in the database or by putting the search inquiry into Google or other search engines.

News Websites

Again, your brokerage site is not the only place to look up stock fluctuations and charts; major news websites usually have real-time displays of these numbers as well. To search, you would enter the ticker symbol in the search bar of the financial section of the website. Also, most internet browsers and search engines have a stock tracking system, and you can just enter the ticker symbol into the engine and get results immediately. If you are looking in the paper for the information, you would go to the finance section of the paper and look for the ticker symbol in the charts. Remember, though, penny stocks are not traded on the major markets so you may not be able to find your company in the paper since it usually focuses on the biggest movers on the market in that time period.

Your Online Brokerage Account

If you are able to get onto your brokerage account that will ultimately be the best place to view tracking information and you can usually change the settings to focus on your purchased stock. The current prices and the most recent trades should automatically be generated and show up on your home screen when you log on, though every website is different. Make sure to check out your broker's help section to get a thorough understanding of all of the additional tools they offer to better and more efficiently track your investments. If your account doesn't offer anything but the basis, you may want to add to another website that will allow you to use these particular tools or look up the cost to increase your membership in your current site.

Online Portfolios

One of the beautiful things about technology is that you don't have to worry about having thousands of sheets of paper in a real portfolio. Online portfolios are sometimes available through your brokerage page but sometimes you will have to create them from an outside source. If you have one of these portfolios, you should be able to log in, click on the tracker tool, enter your ticker symbol and have all the information you need to make educated choices on your investments. These portfolios also give you the capability of entering in stocks and their updated prices depending on how the market sways. Mint is a great online portfolio that is free and also includes an app for your smartphone so you can quickly track from anywhere.

Alerts

Alerts are going to be your best friend when you are playing the stock market but are unable to be watching your investments consistently. Not only should you set alerts for when stocks dip or your stocks rise or fall to a certain point, but you should also make sure to be informed if the companies you invested in end up in the news for any reason. Good news on a company can help you determine whether to extend you deadlines on specific stocks. Bad news about your business can signal that you need to get rid of the stock and quickly. If you are working in stocks that are affected by weather or exact conditions you should also program alerts for any of those issues as well. Unfortunately, natural events and developments in science can hurt companies, and you need to be aware of what is going on.

Understanding Stock Information

You can get alerts and pull up tracking information on your stocks all day long but if you don't understand what you are looking at it is not going to do you any good. You need to know the different stock information so that you are able to make informed decisions about your investments. Some of the tracking information is self-explanatory while other information can be confusing. Also, there is usually a link between all of the information and without individual statistics and information you may be missing an integral piece of the puzzle. When you are missing parts, it is very likely that you could make a mistake in trading that could cost you significant amounts of money. Again, as we have said through this whole book, educating yourself on all aspects of your investments is not only smart but can make the difference between maximizing your revenue and losing everything you put into it.

Interpreting Price Changes

When you are looking at the tracking information, you are going to see the high, low, and closing prices. These numbers indicate how the stock did, on average, for the prior day, the top, low, and final cost of the stock. The 52-week column is going to give you an excellent idea of how volatile that specific stock is. If the latter two prices have a large difference, then the odds are this stock has a greater opportunity for gain but a higher risk for loss. If the numbers are relatively close then that shows the stock as pretty conservative so you may not achieve as high but your likelihood of loss is less as well. The net change tells you the gain or loss of a specific stock for that twenty-four hour time period and is calculated by taking the previous day's closing cost and subtracting it from the current days. There is a plethora of information on this that can be found on the web.

Dividends

The dividends are going to tell you how much a company would pay you to hold one share of its stock for one year. This dividend might rise, fall, or be removed based on the enterprise's performance and status. If a company continually pays out dividends and increases those payouts over time, the company is considered a good choice to invest in. Dividends are either paid out to the shareholders or reinvested in the enterprise. If a company has a plan for substantial growth, they will usually not pay dividends while the businesses that aren't planning growth will pay out. If you are interested in knowing more about a company's dividend history you can calculate the payout ratio which will tell you how much the company has paid out to shareholders and how that has changed over time.

Price-To-Earnings Ratio

The PE ratio or price-to-earnings ratio is the closing price divided by the earnings of outstanding share and represents the investor confidence that the stock will go up in the future. A low price-to-earnings ratio would represent an underdeveloped company which could trigger a possible active investment to make. This rate primarily represents what an investor is willing to pay for one dollar of the current earnings. So for example, if the PE ratio sits at thirteen, then they are will to pay thirteen dollars for one dollar of the current earnings. Theses findings can sometimes be difficult to understand. A high PE means that the company is stable and there is a good chance the stock prices will rise while the low PE means the company has the potential to grow, also showing a possible rise in stock prices. To really understand where a company fits into its industry, compare PE ratios with similar businesses in the same field.

Trading Volume

The trading volume is very simple and represents the number of shares that was traded that day. An unusual increase in a trade's volume may indicate that it is either on the rise or getting ready to go into a slump, either way, research is needed before purchasing any of that stock. If the price increases with the increase in volume then usually that indicates that a stock will be on the rise and vice versa. The trading volume is also the number you will want to look at when you are ready to begin trading stock. It is important to not sell any more than ten or fifteen percent of the trading volume a day. This is a number you don't have to check every day but is pertinent to your choices in investment.

Ratings

Analysts will sometimes put ratings and price targets that show whether they believe the stock will rise or fall in the future. The ratings include buy, sell, or hold and tell investors what the analysts believe they should do with specific stocks. These ratings can easily be found on any of the major market watch sites but remember they are a guess, not information that you necessarily have to listen to and they could still go either way.

Looking For Patterns

A chart pattern is a particular movement in the stock charts that can be analyzed and used to predict how an individual stock will trend in the future. The information is based on current movement as compared to the past flow of that capital as well as the historical outcomes of similar charting paths. Chartists use this information to help investors decide whether they should buy, sell, or hold their current stock in that company. However, this is also a good skill to have when you are looking at your own businesses and deciding on whether to invest. Penny stocks may be hard to determine through patterns since they have limited information, but you can use it as you move into other stock options in the future. Predicting the movement of stocks is just a prediction, and you should never base your decision on whether to buy a stock or not solely on the charts and patterns you discover.

Know The Business

Stocks can be volatile, especially penny stocks, and tend to highly fluctuate over the course of a week so if you want to get a better idea of a stock's tendency, then you need to look at the stock over the process of a week or month and compare those numbers. If the stock has extreme highs and lows over that period, it may not be a stock you want to invest in since Penny stocks only stay with you for several days. You can also tend to find long-term financial stability by studying the company's financial records if they are available. If the penny stock is a new corporation, then this won't help you very much in determining the positivity of the investment.

Day-Trading

Day-trading highly focuses on the very short term for a stock and can be extremely high risk. Day traders run the risk of experiencing severe losses if their bids are incorrect or if the fees eat up all of their return on investment. Technically day traders bank on being able to read the patterns and understanding whether a particular stock will rise or fall but this is extremely hard to do in the short term, and many of these people lost quickly. Though investors in penny stocks aren't considered day traders they essentially do the same thing, look for patterns and buy and trade in a few day period. Day-trading is not recommended in any type of investment strategy, and you could run the risk of losing more than you put in, taking you backward in your pursuit of your goals.

Trends

The simplest type of pattern for anyone to analyze is the price trend. You want to look for growth and decline of a stock price over days or weeks. Remember that just because a stock had a trend in growth does not mean that in the next fifteen minutes it won't have significant loss. Another trend to discover is basing the stocks on economic trends and major news for a company which can both raise the stock price or even make it come crashing down. A good thing to do when studying trends is to take a compilation of these different numbers to base your decision on. However trends are like fortune telling for investors, you never know if you will make the right choice.

Support and Resistance

Support and resistance are two terms that investors use to point out the numbers in which a specific stock does not move below or above. For example, if you have a stock that routinely gets near or to $23, but never goes over it then it has a resistance of $23. Likewise, if a stock never goes under $12, then it has a support of $12. Understanding this trend and how to track it can help you identify the prices in which the chosen stock will not fall under or go over. When you are working with penny stocks, these numbers may not be available due to the amount of time the company had its shares on the market, but you can try to establish it with its last month of numbers at least.

Head and Shoulders

When we say head and shoulders, we are not talking about curing your dandruff. Instead, we are talking about an intricate pattern that investors and analysts use to determine stock shifts. The pattern is formed when the stock reaches a high, or the left shoulder, dips, reaches an even higher high, the head, dips, and then comes back up to a peak not as high as the head, giving you the right shoulder. This trend usually signifies the end of the upward trend of a stock, and it is then predicted to decline in price. In order to determine where you should sell the stock, you can draw a line between the two head points and it will identify the best location to get rid of the stock.

In this chapter, we discussed many pertinent things that will help you to understand the stock market and even help you predict the rise and fall of stocks. All of this information will become helpful somewhere in your investment journey even if you cannot use it in the penny stock industry. To further be able to invest time and money in your future you need to fully understand risk and the other investments to consider in order to diversify your portfolio.

Chapter 12: Advanced Strategies

Chart Patterns

I've explained some basic information regarding chart reading. However, there's deeper info on this that is very useful to analyze all the information these charts have to offer. There are different patterns within the charts and usually this is discovered after years of experience, watching them happening. However, today I'll share those with you. A double peak is a common pattern. This shows an initial peak, which consolidates in a few hours or days, to have a brief down in different period, after we find a new peak. This second peak will turn into a free fall of the stocks' value.

We have a breakout when a stock is surpassing its highest price, turning into one of the most profit generating patterns. Profit generated by a breakout can go from 30% to 200% in a day or a few days. Predicting the breakout can be simple, as key factors like profit declaration, capital structure changes, industry related news either directly or indirectly tend to predict a breakout. However, neither the speed and range of rising can be determined.

Unexpected news

A basic rule is that unexpected news on an industry level can generate an increase in sales and generate a rise of stock prices, as they draw the trader's attention. It's interesting to highlight that while this is a basic rule for stocks, it is further emphasized in penny stocking because being such small companies, information on them is rarely leaked. The charts clearly reflect a very strong peak along with the news of it.

Release of the Financial Information

Unlike big companies, penny stock companies are not deeply studied by analysts, so these news usually do not have a strong background and surface suddenly. What we normally find are inflated numbers as the company's previous stability and a great deal of stocks to determine the truth of the information.

Factors

There are certain factors related to breakouts such as the stock's reliability level, stock volume, stock price, etc. The deeper the stock volume, the more aggressive becomes the peak. Keep in mind that in a market full of people seeking to profit, they will all be aware of these factors. When the stock volume is reduced, this is usually followed by a progressive and slow drop, a seemingly appropriate moment to sell. However, considering the low supply, you can predict a future peak if the shares keep a slow drop or even stop completely, so if someone sold by this moment, they could think about buying again. It is extremely important to analyze the stock volume during the drop or breakout.

Knowing when a breakout is coming is not a simple job, and this is precisely the job that will earn you money, so you have to pay attention to technical details on the charts in order to take advantage of them. how can you find them? Details such as volume rise should trigger your alarms, followed by a company's background investigation as well as its stock charts. Quickly, wandering around chats, forums and financial news websites, look for events related to the company or industry, possible financial info leaks and all the factors we have studied so far.

There are opportunities where all the factors are there, and, however, the breakout does not happen. We can find different reasons such as stock manipulating by the company itself (this can be discovered by the lack of breakout factors), bank manipulation or big players who can buy enormous quantities, producing a peak, drawing small investors so the big fish put his actions on sale during the brief breakout, and obtaining a small percentage, the volume rise during the breakout will make this stop and even make it drop.

To avoid this, a chart study of the company's stocks can give us an idea of the price on which the stocks remain stable and if they are at this stability point, then risk level lowers down, as loss should be at 5% or a similar low number. On the same charts we can determine the usual peaks and put that percentage as a reference for the stock sale.

Studying the usual peaks allows us to establish an earning level and the risk percentage. Buying at the stability point represents little risk, but buying at the moment of a peak and with a possible breakout on the way is a risky move that requires a study of the peak's catalysts, this way we can be in front of one of the aforementioned manipulations.

This way, the best point to buy a stock is when this is close to its stability point and with possibilities of a breakout. Buying at a max of 10% of stability will assure you the avoid of loss and will enable you to take advantage of the next peak. Remember always checking on the information regarding the company, as with the absence of breakout catalysts, this is not necessarily an attractive stock. Also, info such as small volume before a possible breakout shows low probability of a sustained peak because of the traders being uninterested.

Do you remember when we talked about an ideal number for max and min earnings and loss? A lot of times is not about establishing these levees generally, as the pattern developed by a stock during a period of time can show the process of rise and drop of prices, showing the min and max points of stability. According to this information is that you will establish your potential earning and loss numbers.

Keep in mind that patterns are past events with a high tendencies to repeat themselves, but there are a lot of different patterns and you will have to develop your insight to understand them. Always remember that as there are breakouts, there are breakdowns, charts will give you ideas and clues on this but you have to be careful with this.

Breakdowns

How do you predict a breakdown? It turns out to be relatively simple. The same rules that apply to a breakout can be applied here, just inversely. A loss report, a report on low profit, bad news on the industry or company, employees selling stocks on their own... All these are factors that can provoke a breakdown. However, in one way or another, the information I have given to you can help you avoid this, making safe transactions.

However, breakdowns are great opportunities! This is because they are not always caused by events related to the aforementioned factors. The same way as peaks caused by big fishes, this also can be applied to breakdowns. We have insisted a lot throughout the book on the importance's of establishing your maximum loss levels, however, YOU SHOULD NOT use automated systems to do this. When a stock reaches its stability peak and keeps lowering, it is very important to look for catalysts for the drop. If you cannot find any reasons for the price drop, DO NOT SELL. Why not use automated systems to avoid loss? Because these systems are not capable of checking on the news and sometimes cause artificial breakdowns that you cannot take advantage of.

A lot of amateurs establish their stop loss automated systems near the stability peak, causing a rise of the supply volume and accelerating the down of the prices. This is your chance, as, if there are no real reasons, we find ourselves before a fluctuation that reached the peak calculated by traders, which stimulated a down of prices without any real base, and this can predict a coming peak.

Breakdowns are frequently a lot more aggressive than breakouts, so this is a game where you can gain a lot if you keep your eyes open. Sometimes a catalyst can simply be the small stock market. Considering this, you can gain a lot by buying during the breakdown and selling during the stability peak. This can generate even more profit than a breakout, as sales driven by panic will put you ahead and ready for the resurgence of some shares without reason to go down. Something to take in consideration is that a lot of these driven by panic situations happen during the morning (this is not a golden rule but a tendency ruled by statistics).

Chapter 13: Spotting Hot Trends In Penny Stocks

In the world of stock trading, when you see a hot trend, go with it! It makes sense to follow this advice. Of course you have to know when to back off too, but normally if a stock performs well it will continue for some amount of time. Hopefully, it will continue long enough for you benefit from the investment.

Trends are good but how can you spot them and even predict them? These are the eternal questions that plague investors. If they could answer this, then they'd be billionaires. Still, there are ways to spot hot trends in penny stocks. Here are some of the most helpful:

1)Learn to identify price trends. If you see the trend for the past few weeks has been going up, that means shares have a good chance of continuing that increase. On the other hand if it's going down, assume the same only on a decrease. A trend is nothing more than a propensity of moving one way or another for a set amount of time. If you key in on a trend, take advantage of it.

2)Once you identify a trend in pricing with penny stocks, put yourself in the right position to take advantage of it. A general rule of thumb is to purchase when penny stocks are on the way up. Since you know the trend of the penny stock is moving up, ride it! Jump on the investment and hope to capitalize on a good thing.

3)Know when to pull out. The strategy with penny stocks and understanding trends is to know when to end your investment. Any investor knows that to stay beyond your welcome with a stock that is plummeting can mean sure loss. That is what all investors try desperately to avoid. A rule is that all good things must end. That means that even if your penny stock has been outperforming everything else, sooner or later it won't.

4)Check forums. Forums and chatrooms are a great way to stay up to date with what kind of trends to look for. Of course when I say forums I don't mean read what they're saying I mean actually get involved talk to people who have a bit more experience than you. Not only that but when the time comes when you are a professional you can too be the person someone comes to for help. Being part of a community will help you grow much faster than just being all over the place.

Trends can relate to two things: trading volume and share price. For example, let's say a penny stock's share is getting more trading volume for the past 5 weeks. This may be an indicator of increasing volume, which may forecast more investor movement. The prices could soon be rising steadily as a result.

When looking for trends, watch the trading charts. If you see upward movement, the penny stock is on an upswing. If you see downward movement, the opposite is true. Small, or even large, fluctuations can normally be discounted. You want a big picture view when you're looking for how to spot hot trends in penny stocks. Also- remember to widen your snapshot to see a trend. Some trends don't show up with penny slots when looking at a 3-week period; but, when you widen your view to a 3-month period you can capture a valuable trend to capitalize on.

Chapter 14: Techniques Of Trading Penny Stocks: Getting Specific

In this section of the book, we are interested in specific techniques that you can try out to join the ranks of successful penny stocks investors. These techniques are not so easy just the same, it is not easy to make money with penny stocks. But in the world of investing, no path is so clear and no step is so easy. Some may seem so unethical.

Pump and Dump

I have not changed my position on this one. It is still unethical or probably illegal in your country of residence. The fact that this is one of the most popular techniques that is used by a number of people to make money in the stock market is reason good enough for me to tell you about it. This technique is also difficult to make work and more than often lands its users in trouble.

Just buy that stock and then convince that it is worth more than the price you bought it. Once people believe you, sell them at the hyped or inflated price and step away from the trading table. Well, you will make quick cash but you will have compromised your integrity because that is one of the scammers I told you about. Do not try it at home!

Invest in Turnaround Company

There are companies that get up to their feet with much force after suffering huge debts or bankruptcy. Sometimes all that these companies need is extra love and attention. Such companies can surprise especially when a restructuring is done and other people buy the business, which helps get it back on track.

Such companies offer an opportunity for you to over double your returns. It is however difficult to predict a turnaround company and such penny stocks are still risky. Your best hope when using this technique is that you hold the stock until the company turns around and gets back to its normal track. When this happens, you will be able to sell your stocks at a good price. The risks are equally high just as the returns. Sometimes the market forces are unfair and can undervalue a company. When your value analysis informs you so, then you have a real opportunity. Grab it at once.

Dollar Cost Average (DCA)

For beginning investors like you, buying many penny stocks all at once may seem the most prudent thing to do given the commissions and other transactional costs. However, the advocates of DCA caution that this might turn more expensive than if these shares were bought in bits.

DCA is where additional shares are bought at set time intervals regardless of prices or stock activities. This prevents investors from buying large stocks at wrong time when the prices are at their highest. More penny stocks are bought when the prices are low and vice versa. The average price will in turn be very low.

Stop-Loss Orders

This strategy prevents you from suffering the downside while you open your potential to the upside of the market. This strategy entails giving your broker an order to sell your stocks when a percentage price fall is reached in relation to your purchase price. This in essence means that your stock is up for sale immediately your stock price is triggered.

Today's brokers have made this technique easy by offering automated stop-order services. In the absence of this automated stop-order loss, you can have a mental stop-loss order but this can be a daunting task given the tendency of beginning investors to become so attached to their stocks even when it is doing badly. For this to work for you, you have to stick to the strategy without giving reasons or hoping for a turn around.

Position Sizing

This is the perhaps one of the most misunderstood techniques yet quite powerful. It works best for investors with large stock portfolio. It is where an investor limits their purchase of an individual stock to a certain percentage of their portfolio.

If you have a portfolio of say $ 20000, you can say you are buying penny stock A worth $2000. This is 10% of your portfolio. You can then purchase the remaining from other companies. In this way, you limit your losses on a single stock. For small portfolios, this technique may not be profitable owing to commissions.

Just Be Lucky

It is very difficult to predict luck. I think it is one of the abstract things. The proponents of this technique believe that you can buy stocks and hold them until their value is worth it (or swallow a loss out of disgust). In a recent investment forum, one of the speakers told us that there is a simple way to find a good cheap to invest in. you need to be lucky. Really, I do not agree.

In your search for luck, it is important to keep in mind that a company that has low priced stocks has a reason behind it. It could be that the company is financially handicapped or battered and is looking for funds to turn it around. With the use of value investing and technical analyses, you owe it to yourself to find out.

Chapter 15: Buying Stocks

You now know what a stock is and some about the principles behind the market they're traded in, but how do you actually purchase a stock? Fortunately, a trip to the stock market in New York City is not in your near future unless you really want it to be. There are two main ways to purchase stocks.

Brokerage

Using a brokerage is the most common way to purchase stocks. They come in two different styles. Full-service brokerages will offer you expert advice and will manage your accounts, but they do charge a hefty price. Discount brokerages will offer very little personal attention to your portfolio, but they are cheaper.

It used to be that only the wealthy were able to afford brokers because they were expensive and full-service only. When the internet came about, the explosion of online discount brokers also made an appearance. Thanks to the internet, almost anyone can afford to invest in the market.

DIPs and DRIPs

DRIPs are dividend reinvestment plans and DIPs are direct investment plans. These plans are how individual companies, at a low cost, allow a shareholder to purchase stock directly from them. DRIPs are an excellent way to invest a small amount into a company at a regular interval.

Purchasing stocks is not difficult at all. All you have to do is go online and sign up on a reputable website in order to start trading.

Chapter 16: Technical Trends

General range:

General range is a rough idea of how the stock has been performing and the prediction for how it will perform by extrapolating previous lines. Even though this is a rough estimate and has no inclusion of the real market, this graph is useful to evaluate an upper and lower range. Calculating that, you can find the resistance level of the stock. Resistance levels, as told earlier are the true representation of the stock value at that moment. Simply put, General range is where the stock rests. Most of the chaotic volatile trading happens outside of the general range. As soon as the stock gets outside the general range, prepare for some action.

Current range:

Current range usually dictates the current trend of the graph. If the graph has been steadily going up in the past two days, the graph is said to be in uptrend while if the graph is losing value continuously, it is said to be in downtrend. Similarly, two uptrends for every downtrend means the stock price is rising while the consequent is true if the downtrends are more in number than the uptrends. Keep in mind that the graph can always turn the cards upside down. Trend reversal is the term used when the stock shifts the trend instantly and goes into opposite trend for a long time. Trend reversals can be helpful for you because they can help you pinpoint the lowest the stock will go before it rises up and you can buy stock at the lowest and sell when the new trend settles itself for a higher value.

Trading Volume:

Trading volume is the number of shares traded every day by a company. This could be a potential analytic tool if we consider trades of shares as interest in the company. The more the words goes out for a company, the more people start investing and higher the price goes. Conversely, the lesser the interest in the company, the lesser the trade volume and lower share price. Most finance websites give instant results for trading volumes of most companies. Keep checking it out while you invest.

Resistance/Support Levels:

These levels are the stock values the stock will likely to converge at after a bull or bear run. A support level is the value of the stock, which is very likely to be breached downwards while resistance level is the value that the stock is pushing against but can't successfully rise above. It is very likely that both support and resistance levels will be taken on many times each day but it's more likely that the stock will fall back to the last support or resistance value. Both of these points are a good time to cash out the profits because the stock will continue on the same direction but would be ready for deviation very soon. Or simultaneously you could trade again and again near the support and resistance value to gain small profits for many times in a row.

Dips:

Dips in stock trading are the period when the stock drops 20-30% of value suddenly accompanied by a decrease in trade volume. It is the golden time for buying stocks, which makes dips temporary, and this phenomenon disappears in a few hours. The dips do not have any reason for their happening and should not be confused with a panic selloff by the investors.

Collapse:

Unlike dips, which are short lived, a collapse is irreversible and permanent. It occurs when the company has run into a hurdle or is running on fumes. This phenomenon shows no signs of happening and can suddenly occur. Investors continue confusing it with a dip but it never recovers. It happens after a period of share devaluations and the market goes into a downward tremble. A temporary support level is achieved but the graphs sheds value slowly over time.

Spikes:

This process is just like a dip, but in the opposite direction. These short-lived overvaluations are fueled by small events that capture investor interests momentarily. This might include, a lax in economic policies or an FDA approval for a pharmaceutical company. These spikes usually go up 20-30% suddenly, hold for a moment and then get tumbling back because the graphs balances itself to the natural value. A simple way of knowing a short-lived spike is by checking trading volume. It usually gets up two-fold. Spikes are great points to dump stock but keep in mind that almost everyone with the knowledge will be doing the same. The best technique is to sell at the peak and when the value drops for revaluation, buyback. This way you will gain a huge chunk on behalf of your stock.

Growth Spike:

Just like a collapse, this is a permanent change in the trend of stocks. A growth usually takes the stock up by 50-75%. The up flow has obvious reasons behind it and represents an increase in valuation of the company by the investors. Investor might confuse growth spike with a short-lived spike and to get profits, might lose an opportunity for a long-term growth opportunity. A growth spike is characterized by a slow growth over weeks and then a sudden shoot up. Trading volume is also running at very high before the stock shoots up. This lasts indefinitely and represents the next base level of the stock.

Topping out:

The next thing to happen after a growth spike is called a topping out. When a stock sees great improvement in price, investors start cashing out their investments to call it a day. As a result, the graph flat lines for a bit. This flatting slows down the list of buyers while investors keep on selling. The curve now starts to show signs of going down. Anxiety runs in the rest of the investors who start cashing out in the fear of a dip. This, ironically, becomes the reason for a dip because the cashing out gains momentum. The stocks then drop down to a support value and stay there till the next bout of company growth.

For traders, you should analyze the patterns of trade volume to see if the graph is topping out or has stalled for no reason. Trade volume will help you with this. If the volume is getting down, this is definitely a topping out but if those values remain stable and healthy, the graph might be looking forward to the next episode of growth.

Bottom:

This is the point where the stocks are at the lowest in a referenced time frame. This might happen because of a long run up where most of the investors are cashing out in hordes. This is an indication that the stocks are about to see an upward trend. Bottoming out is an excellent opportunity to buy stocks because it could be a sign of reversal of trends or a significant growth. Double bottom is a unique occurrence when the stock hits a bottom rises up soon after and then goes back crashing to similar value before.

Consolidation:

Consolidation is when the stock is neither going up nor going down. It is trading in a limited range without giving much opportunity for investors. For a trader, this shows that a lot of stock is trading hands. Dumping and pumping of stocks have reached a dynamic equilibrium. Consolidation is neither good nor bad for a day trader. What matters is the breaking out of a pattern. As soon as the consolidation period ends, a trend could breakout, which involves furious trading. Either the buyers win or the sellers do. Identify the duration of the consolidation and decide whether you want to buy or sell relatively.

Chapter 17: Advantages And Disadvantages Of Penny Stocks

As a type of equity, a penny stock is often valued below $5. In most cases, the stock price is even below $1. Because major stock exchanges have price requirements, a penny stock can be found listed on the Pink Sheets or Over-The-Counter Bulletin Board. As such, it isn't part of the big indices and is virtually unknown to an investor. Over-The-Counter listing does have popular companies like British Sky Broadcasting, Deutsche Telecom, and Nestle but most companies in the list aren't popular among investors. Analysts only cover the major exchanges so OTC companies remain hidden from prospective investors. Furthermore, most of these companies can't afford the high costs of listing to the more popular stock exchanges. These companies would rather spend on the improvement of their business. Finally, these companies may not have been discovered yet. As such, their prices don't rise significantly enough to get the investors' attention.

Advantages Of A Penny Stock Investment

Many of the large companies today started as penny stocks or have reached penny stock prices at some point. Microsoft had been in the penny stock category when it did stock splits. Currently, small companies may be at the bottom rung of their industries or may be waiting for exposure to have a major breakthrough. Most of these penny stock companies are waiting on the sidelines to be recognized by analysts for their efforts. Once these companies are noticed, they will generate interest from the big investors. As such, a penny stock company can offer a big earning opportunity before it is discovered and recognized.

A penny stock is also considered for its market risk. A lot of things can affect the market like consumer sentiment, government scandals, and natural calamities. Stock investing can be very risky. Big companies like the Citigroup, AIG, and General Motors had to be bailed out during the recent financial crisis. A lot of big companies closed their operations. Any stock company has its dangers. However, the potential reward is also appealing. A penny stock can generate substantial income and may even quadruple profits in a short time.

In terms of percentage gains, a penny stock can be at par with the other large stocks. A stock bought at 50 cents and sold at $1 is actually the same as a stock bought at $50 and sold at $100. Furthermore, it is even more common for a penny stock company to move from 50 cents to $50.

Disadvantages Of Investing In Penny Stocks

A penny stock is highly volatile. It is possible for some large institutional traders to hold the majority of shares which can result in wild price swings. If there are only a few buyers and this large shareholder wants to dispose of his shares, he can lower the price just to sell his shares. On the other hand, if there are so many buyers, he can raise the price significantly in order to realize his profits.

A lot of penny stocks are small companies. Many investors are afraid of investing their hard-earned money with them because of inherent risks they have to face. Some of these companies may not become profitable for so many years. These companies may change management teams a couple of times before they have the perfect match. Some of these companies may die a natural death after a while. After the 2008 financial crisis, a lot of these small companies perished although some large companies also had to be bailed out. But, there are more casualties on the Pink Sheets and OTCBB exchanges.

Because a penny stock is very volatile, it is advised to cash out the gains as soon as possible. A penny stock isn't for long-term investing. It is possible to lose the investment if the investor waits for his target price to be reached. As such, penny stocks are really for day traders or short-term traders. Furthermore, a penny stock is illiquid. This means that there may not be a lot of transactions on a single day. An investor may find it difficult to sell his shares immediately if there no buyers. If this happens, the stock price will further decrease.

There are various ways to mitigate penny stock risks. An investor can use tight stop losses. Furthermore, he must be disciplined enough to sell when it's time to sell in order to lock in his gains or to limit his losses. Penny stock has high risks but it also offers high rewards. Compared to large stock corporations, a penny stock has the potential to generate large profits at a short time. Some big companies can take years to achieve high gains. A hot penny stock can triple its price faster than any large stock. An investor must be armed with the right knowledge, discipline, and tools if he wants to earn from penny stocks.

Penny Stocks Trading

A penny stock provides an opportunity for an online investor to purchase a large number of shares at a low price. Although It may be appealing to some, it is important to note that the price of a penny stock can be manipulated easily. Large stock corporations require billions of dollars to move the price of their stock. With a penny stock, a few hundred dollars can move its stock price. If there's even a small hint of negativity or hype, it can have a huge effort on the stock price. It only takes at least a movement of one penny for a scammer to profit substantially.

A lot of penny stocks aren't listed on any major stock exchange. These stocks are found on Pink Sheets and OTCBB. Actually, these exchanges are referred to as the Wild Wild West of Internet Investing. A lot of experts don't advise investing in penny stocks. However, those investors who still want to take advantage of the substantial earning possibilities that a penny stock offers, they just have to follow some simple rules.

A penny stock investor must heed the regulators' warnings. He can keep track of various releases by the Securities and Exchange Commission regarding penny stock investing. He can make a quick search on the SEC website to gather information about the penny stock company and its officers. In addition, otcMarkets provides a rating for companies in terms of the information these businesses provide to their investors. In terms of quality, otcQX is the highest rating and Caveat Emptor is its lowest rating. He can also check the website of the Over-The-Counter Bulletin Board for similar information about its member companies. For example, OTCBB has a list of Eligibility and Delinquency for those companies which failed to meet its minimum standards.

It is also important for a penny stock investor to practice due diligence. He must check the financial statements of the company. There are websites which offer exhaustive investigative reports on most companies. The investor can read about a particular penny stock company to learn about it. Lastly, there are also penny stocks listed on NASDAQ and NYSE. The investor can opt to invest on this stocks because these are better regulated than the others.

Mitigating Penny Stock Risks

Those individuals who don't know about the perils of penny stock investing often get burned. However, those investors who follow some simple rules in investing often become successful. First, for penny stocks, there are so many of them in major stock exchanges or at OTCBB. It is best to stay away from Pink Sheets because member companies aren't required to meet minimum standards to stay listed. Second, a "hot tip" shouldn't be taken seriously, even if it comes from a friend. A conscientious investor makes it a point to practice due diligence in investing. Third, he mustn't subscribe to free stock picks because these are just a strategy by unscrupulous individuals to lure unsuspecting investors to their trap.

Fourth, the investor is advised to choose penny stocks which are fundamentally solid. This means that he takes his time in checking the financial position and performance of the penny stock company. Fifth, excellent business concepts must be studied. There are stock stories which tend to focus on a business concept as the penny stock's selling point. For the investor, it is best for him to check the feasibility of the concept together with the company's financial position. Lastly, he must ask his questions through the penny stock company's investor relations. He must be able to ask the right questions so that he'll know if the business is legitimate.

Finding Great Penny Stock Investments

A penny stock company must be able to adapt to a growing market. This means that as the market expands, its market share also grows with it. It must be at par with its competitors. By using financial valuation ratios, the penny stock must be able to prove its compelling value. It must be able to adopt strategies to reduce expenses and increase revenues to show that it is serious in attaining profitability. Each member in the management team must have experience in successfully managing past businesses. The penny stock company must respect intellectual properties of other businesses and protect its intellectual assets as well. Its products and services must be highly accepted by its consumer base. Lastly, the penny stock company must implement a solid and effective marketing plan in order to promote the brand.

A penny stock has its advantages and disadvantages. While there are really great penny stock companies, there are also penny stock companies which are used by fraudsters to trick unsuspecting investors. Those individuals who want to earn from penny stocks must be able to separate the legitimate ones from the dubious penny stock companies.

Chapter 18: Tips That Can Get You A Long Way

Penny stock trading is a risky venture, but with the right information in hand and good guidance, you will be able to avoid the risks and dance around the manholes that litter the road to penny stock success.

Here are a few tips that can help you to avoid falling into a schemers' trap, and at the same time ensure that you receive a good profit in every transaction:

Do not believe stories. The world of penny stock trading and investment is full of people whose main goal is to lure unwitting investors to fall into their deceitful scams and schemes. One way of doing that is spreading stories all over the internet that tell of individuals who made it big in penny stocks by doing this and that or visiting sites here and there. Most of the time, these stories are sent through emails and posted in social networking sites, which are platforms that can reach a lot of people efficiently in a matter of time. If ever you encounter these stories in your mail or you come across them in forums, it is best to ignore them.

Focus on good penny stocks only. It is very recommendable that you should put your focus penny stocks that will surely give you profits. Look at how the stock's earnings grow. Make sure that they are consistent and make 52 week highs. They should also have good earnings breakout and should trade in volumes of at least a hundred thousand shares.

Another tip related to selecting good stocks is to lengthen your search time. Duration of four to six is better. This is because stocks that consistently appear in the listings of exchanges are more likely to be consistent performers also, helping you avoid falling for stocks with only short bursts of luck.

Pay no heed to tips. Like stories, tips on penny stocks abound the internet. Mostly, these tips are about when to sell and what penny stocks to sell, and usually are given to people through their emails and distributed penny stock newsletters.

Always look for disclaimers. In connection with the previous paragraph, one way to avoid getting fooled by tips is to look at the disclaimer portion of the newsletter that contained the tip. There is actually nothing wrong with penny stock newsletters by themselves. In fact, they can serve as ways for small growing companies to gain publicity. The thing with them is that newsletter publishers are paid to give these tips and spotlight the company' stock, and most of the time they also print good things about how the company is doing despite that company's very poor performance. To avoid getting fooled, you should read the disclaimers that are printed in the newsletters, usually found in the bottom part. Disclaimers are required by the Securities Exchange Commission to be included in newsletters, and it is there that the real purpose of the tip is indicated.

Get your hands off of fast growing stocks quickly. For an investor who has just started trading in penny stocks, getting your hands on stocks with a large and fast growth that can reach to around 25% is very amazing. Usually, beginners tend to be amazed too much and want to reach a higher return. However, veteran penny stock traders recommend letting go of these kinds of stocks quickly. For one reason, you should grab the chance of benefitting from the stock when it is at its highest performance. Another reason is that stocks with good performance within only just days are more likely to have been subjected to the pumping and dumping scheme.

There are sources that say that shorting penny stocks is a good way to earn more profit. However, shorting penny stocks are best left to the more experienced and professional penny stocks traders and investors. The problem with penny stock shorting is that penny stocks are unpredictable, which can lead you to losing large sums of money instead of gaining profit. Another thing is that it is quite hard to look for penny stocks to short.

Know what stocks to buy. Buying the wrong kinds of stocks will not help you gain any profit, but instead will bring you loss. Experts recommend buying stocks which trade equal to, or more than 100,000 shares per day. Investing in shares that trade in high volume will make things easier for you when you want to get them off your hands. The importance of research again enters here. You must know the volume of the shares traded and the volume of the dollars. Furthermore, buying penny stocks with trading prices below .50 dollars per share is a no-no. You must invest in stocks that are above this price so that you can be liquid when the time for selling comes.

Avoid trading big. Although you need to invest in stocks that trade in high volume for each day, you should also avoid trading at least 10% of that stock's daily trading volume. For example, for a stock that trades 100,000 share volumes, you can buy 10,000 shares.

Chapter 19: Learning The Basics Of Day Trading

Penny stocks have actually proven their worth in these tough times of economic meltdowns. The number of people who make it big in the stock market is increasing by the day and they are not even people who are into stock trading full time. With experience though, most people make a shift towards the dearer stocks that are more promiscuous on delivering higher profits.

But that involves higher risk. The objective should be to maximize profit while minimizing risks. So what exactly do we refer to when we use the term "penny stocks"? The definition of these stocks actually varies over the resource that you use. However, it may be helpful for general information to know that these stocks are steep on speculations but are priced at a dollar each or less. The kind of fluctuation in value exhibited by all of these stocks is really extreme and keeps changing to the minute.

The risk involved is very high. But when high risk pays off, the rewards are often even higher. There are some basic conjectures to trading in them. There's a good time and amount to trade in each one of them. Expertise and experience is the key to success. Don't play too much ahead of yourself. Understand the risks and gain credibility from less risk bearing trades. Only when you are fully confident should you think about stock trading in pennies. Experience is always a great teacher. Time spent in learning and acquiring the tricks of the trade in the stock market is absolutely invaluable.

Their happen to be fluctuations that apparently seem random. But with vast experience, you may expect to be able to read the trends. But you may not always have the patience to keep on toiling. That is why getting a better understanding of the market serves really well. There always exist shortcuts to success just waiting for you to take them. A multitude of methods show the way to analyzing trends but their accuracy is highly questionable. All the tools available predict the future based on the past. However, what the future holds in store may not be anyone's guess.

But as they say, "where there is will, there is a way". Newer methods are being developed for forecasting stock trading trends. Software programs are being put in place by means of which more accurate predictions can be made. Stock trading today has reached unprecedented heights with penny stocks coming into play big time. Some people have even made millions trading them successfully. Unlike old times the way people look at stock trading has also changed. Today all professionals trade stocks in hope of attaining a better life rather than expecting to make a fortune overnight. This has helped too.

Trading in penny stocks tends to attract the interest of newbie investors because it can seem accessible thanks to the small amounts of money needed to make a first purchase. The mistake many make however is having the false hope that they can magically hit it rich with some awesome penny stocks as soon as they get started. They can become greedy, lose all their money very quickly and then become disillusioned with the whole thing.

But if you are reading this then hopefully you won't be one of these misguided investors!

Basic penny stock concepts

The phrases going long and going short describe two of the types of strategies great penny stock traders can follow and we will describe them below now.

Going Long

When people invest in penny stocks and plan to hold on to them watching the share price go up in line with the overall market they are known to be going long. This tactic normally takes a number of years to pay off.

The problem that beginners often do not get their head around is that whilst the market does in fact rise when looked at on a long enough timeline as a whole, this won't always mean that the same will happen to the stocks of individual companies. Investors will at some point lose money because it is a fact that companies go out of business and it is unreasonable to expect otherwise.

It can be quite nerve racking for traders who choose to go long, watching the value of their investments rise and fall in the short to medium term. Assuming their companies manage to stay in business, these investors must stay true to the process and trust that the stock market will in fact continue it's long-term upward trend.

Whilst a lot of money can be made going long, the risks involved with going short can reap much quicker benefits.

Going Short

It is the volatility of the short term that a skilled investor in penny stocks can leverage to their advantage.

Very large amounts of money can be made when investors buy and sell penny stocks over the short term. Believe it or not, it is not unheard of that an investor will buy and sell the same shares a number of times in the same day to turn a profit. But things do have the ability to go downhill fast and investors need to be aware of this risk and be willing to take it in order to experience the potential benefits.

But there is no reason to think that you can not learn all you need to become such a skilled investor to take advantage of the penny stock market in such a way.

Timing is such an important factor when going short and you have a few options when it comes to picking up this skill. Either learn the hard way by making your own mistakes, or take advantage of a number of learning resources that are available to you. One of the ultimate skills you will develop over time is being able to time your transactions, knowing exactly when your stock is about to make a move.

Guide For Day Trading

If you are looking to trade shares in the stock market for quick results and intend to experience the adventures of swift buying and selling of shares day trading is just the thing for you. Day trading is a process of both buying and selling your stocks on the same day in return of a profit or loss.

Trading in stocks is a bit of a gamble as it involves risks as much as gains, especially when you make rapid purchases and sell offs in a short span of time. Sometimes you can make windfall gains in as less as fifteen minutes or may lose as much money in a wrong move in a similar timeframe. Armed with the right kind of knowledge and some expert guidance, you can make this game tilt to your advantage and bring out the entrepreneur in you.

If you are day trading wisely, you can indeed make a fortune much faster than any other profession would allow you to. In order to understand the tricks of the trade, keep these points in mind and get started with day trading successfully to make regular profits.

Do your research

There are several types of software that are available online on a trial basis which can help you filter stocks with preferences such as momentum, volume, trades and much more. You need to make a prudent choice and bank on your knowledge about trading stocks. Instincts too have a role to play, but only after you have the apt knowledge.

Understand the stock market concept

When you invest in a stock, you basically own a part, no matter how trivial or significant in size, of a company. The deeper understanding of the companies will therefore help you trade with success. It is therefore important to understand the fundamentals on which the company operates on.

Learn to buy and sell your stocks:

In order to buy or sell your stocks you shall need an online broker account. There are several websites available for free trials online that shall help you go through the process with ease and cost you little money if you choose your website with care.

Learning to read stock quotes

While this may seem difficult for a beginner to grasp the help of a website to break down the technicalities of stocks is a must. Terms like "last price", "previous close", "open", "bid/ask", "volume" and "change" are the basics which you should learn before getting started.

Learning what moves the stock price

When there are a lot of people buying a share of a particular company and not selling it, it is sure to make the stock price go up. The stocks of any company are finite in number and when there is excessive demand for it, the price automatically rises. Learning the techniques and the working of the same is significant for a beginner before starting to trade.

Learn rules for day trading penny stocks

A lot of day traders make huge amount of gains by dealing in penny stocks. These are stocks of smaller, lesser known companies that rise and fall alarmingly. Although you can make a lot of money by trading in penny stocks you could lose a lot of money too! If you intend to trade in penny stocks, you have to learn how to read the signs for a big gain or a big fall ahead and book your profits at the right time.

Simple Rules For New Traders

Investing in penny stocks is a great way to make a large amount of money in a short amount of time, but only if you are equipped with the proper repertoire of skills required to effectively navigate the immense sea of information and deceit that is the small-cap marketplace.

If all that it took to make +100% gains each day in the stock market was to check your email in-box, Twitter feed, or favorite financial message board or execute a quick Google search, the world would be free of poverty and there would be no need for this article. Unfortunately, that is not the case.

This piece is certainly not a comprehensive guide to penny stock investing and reading it will not automatically guarantee that you become the next millionaire investor. However, it should make it less likely that you are "duped" by unscrupulous promoters and are more likely that you make more informed decisions before wagering one penny of your hard earned money.

Rule #1 Know the nature of the beast before you invest. The world of penny stocks is often referred to as the "Wild West" of the financial marketplace and rightfully so! Risk awaits you around every corner and the landscape is chock full of liars, cheaters, thieves, and worse! Most companies won't be around in a year or two and over the course of their existence will employ numerous management teams, execute multiple name changes and reverse stock splits, and target a variety of "hot" markets with "breakthrough" products or technologies.Therefore, it behooves you to take everything you hear as a half-truth - at best!

1a. Risk & volatility: Penny stocks are some of the riskiest and volatile investment products available in the U.S. Price swings are fast and furious at this end of the financial marketplace and what is actively traded today could go dormant tomorrow.

1b. Take your time/consult a pro: While you may be able to get away with checking your 401K every month or perhaps each quarter, penny stock investing is a far more precise art that requires more frequent scrutiny and greater safeguards on your behalf. So, if you don't have the time to conduct proper due diligence and closely monitor your investments or the money to hire a professional that does, this is not a place for you to play.

1c. Be cautious with long positions: Because change occurs to so rapidly in the wonderful land of penny stocks, I generally refrain from holding onto shares for long period of time, except for in a few cases when I have been involved with the company prior to it become a public entity or have a close relationship with the management team and a deep understanding of the company's business plan and core markets. The way that I like to think about it is that if I would not go to work for a particular company tomorrow and accept restricted stock in lieu of cash or would not loan the company my own money for 6 months, I wouldn't take a long position in their stock.

1d. Practice, Practice, Practice! If you are new to trading, I strongly suggest writing down your trades for a period of time before actually logging them with a real-life broker. This will give you a chance to develop an effective strategy and learn what works and what doesn't without risking any money.

Rule # 2 Welcome to the casino: Never risk more than you can afford to lose: While it's not out of the ordinary for penny stocks to experience gains of more than 1,000% in just one day, most don't and the ones that do typically don't hold gains for too long. In fact, many of the fastest gainers end up dropping to pre-run levels faster than they rose in the first place. It's unbelievable, but some folks will risk everything including their lunch money, this month's rent or even retirement savings on a whim in hopes that a thinly-traded, highly speculative investment in a micro-cap company that is not even required to file a financial report with securities bodies to prove that they are actually doing what they claim.

Much like sports betting, the investor can drastically improve their chances of success by learning as much about the game and its participants, but no matter how much knowledge is acquired, there will always be elements beyond your control that ultimately dictate the outcome. Just like you can't jump on the basketball court and drill a 3-pointer to secure your bet on the NBA Finals, if you own a small percentage of a small-company - which is typically the case for most penny stock investors - you have very little impact on what happens to share price. Also, much like betting, one should never wager more capital than they are comfortable losing and should always be prepared to lose their entire investment. It's quite simple, actually: Don't bet what you don't have!

Rule #3: Always Book Profits When They Are Available - This is where greed comes in to play: Most investors would be tickled pink if their portfolio gained 5% to 10% over the course of the year - let alone a single stock - especially since the beginning of the recent economic downturn. But for some reason - and this absolutely kills me - everybody wants to be the Great Bambino and swing for the fences when it comes to penny stocks. Time and time again, I see investors failing to book profits on their small-cap investments which have gained 20%, 50%, 100%, or sometimes much more. Don't be one of these people!

3a. Use trailing stops: If you're lucky enough to have one of your picks generate some substantial returns, always focus on recovering as much of your initial investment as possible first. Then you can reevaluate the situation and decide if the same set of circumstances that influenced you to buy initially are still present or if you are better yet going back to the drawing board and identifying new prospects. The most effective way to do this is to set trailing stops: If you purchase a stock at $.01 and it doubles to $.02, set a trailing stop at $.018 to protect your investment if you don't get out completely. By doing this you are able to maximize your profits and never lets gains degenerate into losses.

Rule #4: Use Limit Orders & Find a Broker That Uses Stop-Loss Orders. While this might seem like a no-brainer, it could be the difference between losing your investment or doubling it. In a market where a fraction of a penny can represent thousands of dollars of profit or losses, you need to be absolutely certain that you are buying and selling where you want to be and not where the market wants you to. This is why it's imperative to always use limit order versus market orders. Decide on a price that you feel comfortable and don't sway from it, not matter what!

4a. A Stop-Loss Order is designed to help minimize losses or protect profits and is typically set at roughly 10% to 20% lower than your entry price. Just like with your Limit Order, you need to put your emotions on the shelf and pick a firm price where you intend to press the "eject" button. If you follow this one little piece of advice, you'll be ahead of 99% of the other penny stock investors out there and should never have to complain about getting scalped in the micro-cap markets. Remember, every massive loss started out as a small one.

Rule #5: Looks Before You Leap! (Conduct Extensive Due Diligence). Another common sense rule, but it's amazing how many people fail to conduct even the most basic level of due diligence before executing a trade. You need to be aware of what you are buying before you pull the trigger and unfortunately, there is substantially less trustworthy information available on penny stocks than on larger companies. For this reason, you need to get creative if you want to profit in the crazy world of penny stocks.

Financial reports, press releases, corporate websites, social media, BBB ratings, online message boards, stock charts and technical analysis websites, news and industry reports are all essentials, BUT don't forget to step offline as well and call up the company's management or investor relations firm to learn more. If you happen to live nearby, stop by the office in your spare time. Also, don't hesitate to contact an investment professional.

5a. Use newsletters & blogs as a tool, not a comprehensive source of information: Most penny stock-centric investment newsletters tend to accentuate the positive about the company of focus and for good reason, they are more or less a paid advertisement. Just like you won't see a Pepsi commercial telling you that too much sugar will make you fat, the firm being paid thousands of dollars to introduce a penny stock to investors isn't going to "bash" their client. While I see nothing wrong with such pieces, so long as they are properly disclosing compensation, most fail to mention, yet alone elaborate on downside risk, aside perhaps from the super small print at the bottom of the ad.

Even non-compensated sources tend to impart their trading rationale - whether it supports a short or long position - and not focus too much on the other side of the argument. Again, there's nothing wrong with this because ultimately YOU are responsible for scoping out both sides of the fence and in turn making the most informed decision possible.

5b. Use your head: Before I make a trade, I like to envision myself in the future after a losing trade: I'm OK with the loss if I got an email about company XYZ and then went on to comb through the filings, check out past corporate press releases as well as the website, looked into the BBB rating, read up on XYZ's core markets, studied the chart, spoke with an investment professional and then took a position. However, how dumb do I sound if I picture the future me saying "I got an email on XYZ and read their awesome press release and then placed an order for 1,000,000 shares"?.

5c. Track & Leverage Paid Promotional Campaigns: Some of the biggest penny stock runs over the course of history have been driven not by rock-solid underlying fundamentals but rather by big-budget investor awareness programs. By understanding the dynamics of these projects you can learn how to profit from them, both on the way up and the way down.

There are some very good promotional firms out there with a proven history of updating their followers before penny stocks take off. These entities have amassed thousands of dedicated followers that faithfully check their email in-boxes each day and act upon the advice contained in the messages they receive. The end result here is massive buying power, which you can use to your advantage. A great way to sniff out these campaigns is to do a quick Google search for firms that promote penny stocks and/or message boards that track paid marketing programs.

Chapter 20: The Habit Of Courage

They say stock trading is not for the faint of heart. One habit that you really need to develop to become a highly successful stock trading is the habit of being courageous. To feel fear is normal when you are faced with adversity. But that fear should not paralyse you. Even in fear, you can still move forward. Most people are afraid of heights not because of the height itself but of the fear to fall. That is a built-in self-preservation device that we have. Most investors are afraid to invest in stocks not because of the stocks itself, but because they fear to lose. But in stock trading, you would definitely face lots of adversities. There would be falls. There would be losses. There are heights to climb and the higher you go, the higher the possibility of the fall. Train your heart therefore not to be afraid to fall and lose.

Some people would simply avoid any form of risks. If that is your stand, you are not fit to do stock trading. There would always be risks in stock trading. Always. Actually, the higher the risks, the higher the possible gains. But of course, the higher the fall too, just in case something bad happens. You must be ready for everything. You must be a risk taker. You must not be afraid of risks. Actually, you must welcome them. Because if there are no risks involve, if a certain trade is 100% risk free, then that would be a scam. There are no guarantees here, always remember that.

One thing is very sure with stock trading – there are always risks and losses involved. Nobody can ever claim a 100% risk-free investment in stocks. Be wary of agents telling you that you got nothing to lose. That is a clear signal that you are about to lose something.

You will definitely experience losing in stock trading. But losing does not necessarily mean that it will traumatize you or that the amount of money is huge or it will be your end. Losses are not always detrimental. Most of the time, the lessons you get from these help you become the kind of stock trader that succeeds.

In spite of all the possibilities of losses, successful traders stay with this kind of investment because the gains supersede the losses. Actually, the reality of losing can be a blessing in disguise. This makes the trader more accepting when the inevitable of losing money comes. And it also makes a trader more appreciative when gains are acquired.

One thing that is very evident among the new stock traders is the presence of fear. It is almost tangible. You can smell, hear, see, and touch fear when there are rumours of market instability, which by the way is a daily rumour. Courage will help you survive when there is fear everywhere. Courage would help you lose the fear that threatens you every time. Instead, confidence would take the place of fear.

When you are fearful, it affects your decision-making skills. You tend to do things you would not normally do when you're confident of something. Courage would give you a calm heart and a clear head to decide what to do when chaos is all around. Be courageous at all times. This is one habit of a successful trader that you must strive to develop.

Chapter 21: Penny Stock Analysis Techniques

Analyzing stocks is very important. You have to analyze them through different lenses to see if they make good investment vehicles. In this chapter, we will look at the basic types of analysis that you can use.

Fundamental analysis

Fundamental analysis is the analysis of the basic financial health of the company. You will have to acquire and go through some important documents. At a minimum, reputable companies will at least put out a quarterly report. However, many companies chose to keep their shareholders informed even more frequently than that, on a monthly or biweekly basis. Most of these reports are open to the public. If you cannot find them, you can certainly request a copy from the company in question.

Income statement

This method requires understanding in detail all the income that you receive on a monthly basis through your company. As you know, it can come in the form of operating and non-operating incomes. Operating income is what the company earns by selling the products and services they produce, so it is a direct result of their work that earns them their operating income. On the other hand, non-operating income refers to money that the company earns by means other than product and service sales, so a company can earn non-operating income by selling its possessions such as furniture, televisions etc. If you spot something unusual, such as the company selling a lot of their possessions all at once, it might indicate a financial crisis that they are going through. You must further investigate it before making an investment.

Balance sheet

The balance sheet is a very common financial document that any company maintains to showcase their company's health. A balance sheet helps record many calculations, such as debts that they owe, liabilities that they have, assets that they own, etc. As the name indicates, a balance sheet shows all of these different aspects of the company on a balanced summary, with the income and expense sides balancing out to the same number. When you go through these numbers, you must check if the company has enough assets to counteract the liabilities. If they don't, it means that their stocks will not work well in the long run. On the other hand, if the company has a lot of assets and just a few liabilities, it is a good company to invest with. Remember that companies put out balance sheets every quarter and you have to go through all of them.

Cash flow statement

This is a statement that indicates the total amount of cash that is flowing in and out of the company. A cash flow statement shows the expenses and income that the company has. Based on those two figures, you can tell if a company is faring well or not. A cash flow statement is a great tool to use when you wish to understand the financial health of a company. As opposed to a balance sheet, a cash flow statement is shown in a chronological format. This can be helpful, as it gives you a better idea if there are any rhythms that the company follows. Looking at this report, you can find out if there is a particular time of year in which buying or selling stock would be the most profitable.

These are the different legal papers that you have to go through to check the overall financial health of the company. If you think the company is doing well financially, you can consider investing in it, but not before going through its technical details.

Technical analysis

The next type of analysis is known as technical analysis, which deals with understanding the trends that a stock will follow based on the trends that it has been following in the past.

Obviously, you will have to go through the trends to analyze and understand them effectively. Here are the different types of trends that you have to study when considering a stock.

Direction

The very first thing to look at is the direction in which the stock is moving. Stocks usually move in a predisposed position, which might be up or down. If your stock is moving up and down within equal intervals, it is a good stock to pick. Balanced stocks make for great investment choices. But if your stock has reached its peak point when you plan on investing, you must be careful as its price might start to fall down. You will be running a risk by investing in something that has reached an all-time high. On the other hand, if the stock has reached a low point, chances are high that it will start to rise, so it would be great for you to invest in such a stock. However, remember that neither of these assumptions might turn out to be true, which means that it is tough to generalize. You have to observe several graphs in order to understand price behavior. Graphs such as the candlestick graph can be a great indicator of what direction a stock is going in and when the best time for buying or selling would be.

Speed

The next thing to check is the speed at which the stocks are moving. All stocks will move up and down at a particular speed. This speed determines whether the stock is heading up or down and how fast will it reach the two extreme points.

You can draw 4 points on the graph that will stand for waves 1, 2, 3, and 4. These will help you read the graph better and understand how the trend is occurring.

Now suppose wave 1 and wave 4 are overlapping. This means that the stock is undergoing a correction phase and the two will experience similar values. Most people wait out correction phases in order to allow the price to settle down.

If you think a stock has moved up too fast, you must understand that it will also fall back down just as fast. This can be a telltale sign that the stock is extremely volatile and you must invest in it with caution. Penny stocks are known for this sort of rapid change, so you will first want to try your hand on some more reliable stocks. However, with experience, even speedy stocks can be invested in successfully.

Distance

The next aspect to check is the distance that the stock has covered. It is possible for a stock to surpass its all-time high and keep breaking records. This mainly happens when favorable news about the company breaks out. You will see that the stock is moving higher and higher and then stagnates at a high point. On the other hand, a stock can also move the other way and reach an all-time low. This is most likely when some unfavorable news has broken about the company and the price of the stock is going downward.

Chart patterns

Reading a stock's chart pattern takes into consideration the technical analysis factors discussed above. There are certain frequent patterns that can be very useful indicators as to the strength and viability of a company for investment purposes.

If you keep a detailed journal and enjoy swing trading, creating your own charts may also be a valuable asset to your penny stock endeavor. Any types of charts or graphs are extremely helpful, as they tell you in one glance what words would take a paragraph or more to explain.

Clean chart

A clean chart is one where there is a very clear trend in the pattern of the stock's share price. Either the share price has consistently decreased or consistently increased. It is recommended that you always stick to investing in companies with clean charts because it is much easier to read the trends and make an educated decision as to whether the company is a good investment.

Each of the chart patterns discussed in this section has a messy counterpart. Overall, a messy chart is unhelpful because it does not provide a pattern that will offer a reasonable analysis of the company's share price history and therefore will not assist in predicting future share price trends. Charts that portray trends and averages will always be better than charts that are too detailed to do so. After all, with a chart the goal is to see the forest, not the trees.

Clean bullish

If the trend shows an increase in share prices, this is a bullish trend and is a positive indicator of the financial strength of the company. Be aware of stocks that have bullish trends that are too clean, though, as this can be an indication that there may be some manipulating of the company's share price going on.

Clean bearish

When a company's share price has decreased consistently, this is called a clean bearish trend. Generally, this will be an indication that the company is not doing well financially, and you may wish to avoid investing in such a company. On the other hand, a company that has a clean bearish trend can be a great opportunity for short-selling if you are interested in that type of activity.

Clean breakout

A clean breakout chart shows a company's share price fluctuating within a fairly well-established range, followed by a sudden sharp increase. For anyone interested in penny stock trading, this type of pattern is perfect because, if you purchase shares just as the breakout is starting, you can make a significant profit.

Clean breakdown

As with the clean breakout chart, in a clean breakdown chart, the share's price will fluctuate within a fairly consistent range until there is suddenly a significant decrease. A breakdown can be the result of negative news about a company, or some other event that causes investors to want to sell their stock. If a company's stock starts to break down, you should probably consider selling unless you have reason to believe that the breakdown will be temporary.

However, a breakdown can also sometimes be the result of stop loss orders. If a company's share price fluctuates within a fairly well-established range, there will probably be a fairly clear appropriate stop loss order point that will be chosen by many investors. If the share price happens to hit that point, all of those stop loss orders will be activated because it is an automatic process. Once that occurs, the share price will decrease even further because of the sudden mass exodus of investors.

If you look at a company's chart and see either a clean breakout or a clean breakdown, do some (quick) research into the possible reasons behind the change and decide whether it is a good time to sell or buy, as applicable.

Clean cup and handle

While this may sound like a table setting, a company with a clean cup and handle chart can potentially be a great investment opportunity if you play it right. A cup and handle pattern is when a company's share price rises and then falls over a fairly short period, after an extended period rises again into a breakout. If you time it right, purchase the stocks at the correct time, and wait it out long enough, you can make a substantial profit when the second price rise occurs.

Clean double top

A clean double top chart pattern is essentially the same as the cup and handle, but in the double top there is no breakout of the share price – it simply increases significantly but within the fluctuation trends of the stock. As with the cup and handle, if you time your sale of the stock properly, you can earn significant revenue from this investment.

In addition to these, there are many other things that you can look into, such as the general trend that the stock is following on a monthly basis that will tell you when it will rise and dip. Having proper knowledge about this will help you predict stocks well and invest safely.

Remember that the fundamental and technical analyses are on two different planes, which do not converge. This means that a fundamental analyst need not necessarily be a technical analyst and vice versa. If you wish to properly understand how the company is going, you will have to indulge in both these types.

Hopefully this chapter has helped you understand the different ways in which you can analyze penny stocks to help you improve upon your investments. In the next chapter, we will be taking a look at trading penny stocks as a day trading process.

Chapter 22: Finding Your Broker

In this final chapter, you'll learn about the different types of penny stock brokers out there, and what kind of services they can offer you. This should be very helpful to you when you decide to hire a penny stock broker. Like the previous chapters of this book, this chapter will be geared towards helping you understand the pros and cons of hiring a stock broker once you decide to invest in penny stocks. In other words, you'll discover crucial information that will aid you in making the best decisions based upon your personal needs.

Nowadays, the internet has taken over and completely changed the investment business, leaving many full-service brokers out of jobs, although, interestingly, the percentage of people hiring a broker hasn't experienced a drastic decline. Before the internet made it possible to contact brokers through email or online chats, investors had to call brokers on the phone when they wanted to make a trade, and the commission of the broker was quite bigger than commission rates these days.

Today, the full-time service brokers are now discount brokers. The commissions they make are low – from $5 to $20 per trade, and they use many online tools as well as accounts, which helps them research and trade stocks. When you choose the discount broker that meets your needs, you can, instead of entering your buy and sell choices over the phone, do it faster and easier through the internet. If you decide to call over the phone instead, however, you will be charged a bigger commission by the broker, probably a double fee. When you use a discount broker, you limit the services you could have received by using a full-service broker.

What to Look For in a Broker

When searching for a penny stock broker, you should pay attention to their characteristics. You want the broker you have picked to meet your exact goals, to have similar interests, and to willingly embrace the strategies you feel comfortable with. For example, if you decide to invest a small amount of money, let's say a couple of hundred dollars, you should hire a broker who doesn't require a big balance to open an account. This means you won't need a precise sum of money in your account in order to get started. If trading is what you like and you invest more of your time into this route, then you should find a broker that requires the lowest amount of commission per share, since you'll be using your broker's services quite frequently.

Some of the qualities that you should look for in a penny broker include the following:

A minimum charge to open an account.

Don't apply penalties if the account balance is low.

Commission fees based upon each trade.

The ability to trade on more than one market.

Online account with friendly, easy to use trading interface.

Able to contact easily through both email and phone.

Offers analysis and research tools.

Executes trades fast.

Well-rounded with somewhat extensive client base.

It is up to you to decide and pick which of these qualities mean the most to you. Researching potential brokers will help you choose the best discount broker for you. The qualities that you are looking for when choosing a broker depend upon what you are planning to trade. If you choose a broker for large, blue-chip shares, he will not be so good for trading penny stocks. To trade penny stocks, look for a firm in which the required balance for opening an account is small and offers low per-trade commission rates. Before hiring a broker, ask him about his commission schedule. You may be able to find this type of information by email or online—you need this information in order to know how much you will be charged per trade. You should also find out if there are bonus fees for shares that are trading at a low price.

If you are a new investor, find yourself a broker that will provide you will helpful information, online tools that are easy to use, charts that are interactive, and frequent price alert notifications. Almost every discount broker will provide financial analysis and research tools once your account is set up and ready to go. However, if you are already doing great with the analysis and research tools and you want to try using more advanced ones, you will be charged an additional fee. These more advanced services may sound appealing on the surface, but you will probably do just fine with the free ones available to you. There's really no need for overly fancy electronic tools. In fact, there are a lot of things you can use for free: high-quality charting websites, financial information with price quotes, and additional information from trustworthy sources and resources. Consult with your broker to find out more information, as the services each discount-broker offers will differ to varying degrees.

Direct Access brokers are another category of professional brokers you may encounter during your time in the stock and investing world. They get their name because they give their clients direct trading access online or equip their clients with unique computer software made especially for electronic trading. Direct Access Trading, also known as DAT for short, will give you the chance to directly trade your securities within professional financial markets.

With the Direct Access Trading you can:

Skip over confrontations with retail brokers and jump directly into the actual trading process itself.

Access trading desks like NASDAQ Total View, as well as smart trading software.

The options you receive if you decide to take the Direct Access Trading route depends upon you and your broker.

The web-based version of DAT that is offered by brokers for the financial markets is slow and unpredictable. If you are a trader who trades short-term or daily, you should work towards avoiding the web-based DAT. If you are a penny stock trader, you should, again, not bother with DAT and its internet version because:

You will not be trading in fractions

The trades you have will not be time-sensitive,

Executing your orders through a reliable online discount broker will be a quicker, more efficient process.

There are, of course, a multitude of other advantages that come with Direct Access Trading and working with Direct Access brokers. That is, with DAT, you:

Have access to the Electronic Communication Network (ECN). On ECN, everyone trades as equals, since user's identities are kept hidden. This means that whether you are a novice or professional, retail broker or broker-dealer, and a firm or specialist, you're on the same playing field, so to speak, as everyone else. The only specific information you receive with ECN relates to the current trades that are taking place or the trades that have taken place recently in the past.

Have access to black pools. Black pools are similar to ECN, though they differ in one major way—their systems are closed (private). This means that within black pools, traders are not only anonymous, but also unobservable. You don't have access to information relating to what other people are trading. Like its name suggests, clients are left in the dark. Public markets, too, have no clue about the trades that are happening among black pools.

Access to auction markets. You are able to do direct trading on auction markets like NYSE with a Designated Market Maker or specialist.

The advantages of DAT don't end here, however. The following is a brief but comprehensive list that details many more of the advantages you'll discover through DAT:

Speedy trade executions.

Streaming of charts, real-time quotes, and information about the stock.

Complex portrayal of technical indicators on charts in real time.

Full trade control over your trading on the markets.

Minimized costs with trades under 1,000 shares per order.

Ability to lower your broker costs to a minimum if you take advantage of the ECN adding liquidity, which creates a limited order of buying and selling.

SOR's software automatically finds the best financial markets (NYSE, NASDAQ, many ECNs) and others when your stock is trading in order to find the perfect price for your desirable stock within a few seconds time.

IPA software in which you can input your own strategies to help find stocks.

Ability to see the history and the depth of the trading stock on a multitude of price levels.

Ability for the SA software to be programmed to be more productive over time. This helps you achieve the result you want **now**, and helps you place trades automatically **after** programming and reprogramming.

There is, of course, a downside to this software. Like most things in life, DAT doesn't always work out the exact way we want and need it to. This is due to the fact that broker-dealers manipulate the market, which then creates false signals. If you are a trader and decide to hire a

Direct Access Broker, you should know that many of these brokers will not be the best to work with if you are 1.) A trader who is not that active in the market, 2.) A trader who mainly trades in penny stocks, or 3.) A new or long-term trader.

Upgrading Your Broker

There may be a time when you will want to upgrade your broker; don't be afraid to do so. If the current penny stock broker you have doesn't meet your needs, you can always look for a new one. In fact, you should never hesitate in doing so. There are plenty of discount-brokers available for hiring, most of whom are happy and eager to take on new clients and work toward meeting your own personal needs and interests.

Changing brokers can, however, be troublesome at times, and the broker you currently have may not make the change easy for you. Keep in mind, though, that changing your current broker if he is not meeting your needs is worth the added effort in the end. It's also important to note that it is not necessary to use a single broker for all of your trades and investing needs. Actually, many investors have at least one brokerage account. For example, you might make an account only for the tools the firm offers, make another account to pursue actual penny stock trading endeavors, and yet another account to use when trading large equities only. As always, pursue the routes that fit your personal needs the best, and always find a broker you trust and feel comfortable around.

Conclusion

Thank you again for taking the time to read and review this book!

Throughout this book, we've delved into the world of the penny stock market and learned about the various advantages and disadvantages when trading in penny stocks. Having completed this book, you should have a better, more informed understanding about the big risks but big profit potentials available to those who journey into the world of stocks and investing, particular with penny stocks and pink sheets. As you've recently discovered, just like with any trading, there are plenty of upsides and downsides with penny stocks and trading. Learning and understanding these pros and cons will only make you a better trader and investor.

After you gained a general understanding for what is needed in terms of penny stocks in the first chapter, you then learned about deeper, more complex topics. This is where our discussion about technical analysis came in—you learned how to interpret financial charts and patterns, along with how and when to protect yourself while trading and investing in penny stocks. Following this, we covered all of the general market basics—the strict OTC markets, the OCTBB, and NASDAQ exchanges. We explored the role penny stocks play in three similar but also uniquely different countries around the world—the United States, Canada, and England.

We also examined and discussed pink sheet trading and outlined some somewhat simple but highly efficient trading strategies that you might find useful throughout your future involvement with penny stock trading and investing. You also should have gained a greater understanding about the role of brokers, brokerage accounts, and brokerage firms, the services each has to offer, and the pros and cons that are tied with each category.

Trading and investing in penny stocks can be a very unpredictable interest, hobby, or even career, but it can also be very exciting and highly rewarding. If you are an investor who has a good temper, clear mental state, a great deal of patience, an eye for numbers and predictions, and is looking for a highly rewarding challenge, then penny stocks are the perfect trading stock for you. Take your time and return to specific chapters throughout this book we you're in need of some help or simply need something to reference during your future buying, selling, trading, and investing endeavors. Use the knowledge and the research you've learned here to make your penny stocks investing and trading future brighter, bolder, and successful.